The 1619 Project Myth

The 1619 Project Myth

By Phillip W. Magness

INDEPENDENT
INSTITUTE

Copyright © 2025 by Independent Institute

An earlier version of this book was published in 2020 by The American Institute for Economic Research under the title *The 1619 Project: A Critique*

"The 1619 Project's Confusion on Capitalism" reprinted courtesy of *National Review*
"The 1619 Project Unrepentantly Publishes Junk History" and "Hulu's 1619 Project Docuseries Peddles False History" reprinted courtesy of *Reason*

All rights reserved. No part of this book may be reproduced or transmitted in any form by electronic or mechanical means now known or to be invented, including photocopying, recording, or information storage and retrieval systems, without permission in writing from the publisher, except by a reviewer who may quote brief passages in a review. Nothing herein should be construed as necessarily reflecting the views of the Institute or as an attempt to aid or hinder the passage of any bill before Congress.

ISBN: 978-1-59813-409-4
eISBN: 978-1-59813-411-7

Cataloging-in-Publication Data on file with the Library of Congress

Independent Institute
100 Swan Way, Oakland, CA 94621-1428
Telephone: 510-632-1366
Fax: 510-568-6040
Email: info@independent.org
Website: www.independent.org

Cover Design: John Caruso
Interior Design: Mike Mott

10 9 8 7 6 5 4 3 2 1

Contents

	Preface to the Updated Edition	*vii*
	Preface	*xi*
1	How the 1619 Project Rehabilitates the "King Cotton" Thesis	1
2	The Anti-Capitalist Ideology of Slavery	7
3	How Capitalist-Abolitionists Fought Slavery	13
4	The Statistical Errors of the Reparations Agenda	19
5	Fact-Checking the 1619 Project and Its Critics	23
6	The Case for Retracting Matthew Desmond's 1619 Project Essay	35
7	A Comment on the "New" History of American Capitalism	43
8	The New History of Capitalism Has a "Whiteness" Problem	65
9	What the 1619 Project's Critics Get Wrong About Lincoln	73
10	The 1619 Project: An Epitaph	81
11	Should K–12 Classrooms Teach from the 1619 Project?	87

12	Down the 1619 Project's Memory Hole	95
13	The Suicide of the American Historical Association	103
14	The 1619 Project Unrepentantly Pushes Junk History	111
15	Hulu's *1619* Docuseries Peddles False History	125
16	The 1619 Project's Confusion on Capitalism	131
17	The Tooth-Fairy Economics of Slavery Reparations	141
	Notes	145
	Index	161
	About the Author	167

Preface to the Updated Edition

WHEN I PUBLISHED the first edition of this book four years ago, I believed that the scholarly discussion about the *New York Times*'s 1619 Project had largely run its course. I intended the book to serve as a resource for readers seeking a critical but measured analysis of the controversies stemming from the newspaper's August 2019 magazine edition of the original project.

A number of other rebuttals of the 1619 Project appeared in print around the same time, offering additional insights to the discussion. My contribution differed in two ways, owing largely to my own background as an economic historian. First, I was the only critic who focused primarily on the 1619 Project's economic arguments, and particularly its attempts to link modern American capitalism to slavery. Other historians similarly noted the shortcomings of Matthew Desmond's chapter on this subject in the original series, while concentrating the bulk of their analysis on the faulty historical claims of Nikole Hannah-Jones's lead essay. As I noted at the time, Desmond's argument formed the crucial link between Hannah-Jones's faulty claims about the American founding and her prescriptive policy goals in the present day, specifically large-scale income redistribution and slavery reparations.

Second, while I was largely critical of the 1619 Project's aims, I also offered narrow defenses of areas where it had been unfairly attacked. For example, a number of historians were too quick to dismiss the original project's discussion of Abraham Lincoln's colonization initiatives during the Civil War by portraying them as a minor component of his presidency. I also noted that many of the original project's essays on literature, music, and culture contained reasonable synopses of their authors' scholarly contributions and did not suffer the defects of the essays by Hannah-Jones and Desmond.

Politics breathed a new life into the 1619 Project debate in the months before the 2020 presidential election, leaving the discussion about its scholarly merits and faults significantly worse for the wear. While the project's politician-critics on the right, including President Donald Trump, injected it into the circus of political campaigning, Hannah-Jones stooped to this challenge and joined the ensuing clown act. Facing backlash over her previous assertion that 1619 should replace 1776 as America's founding date, Hannah-Jones went on national television and told a lie by insisting that she never made this claim.

In this new edition, I include additional essays that I wrote in response to Hannah-Jones's lie, which also led to the discovery of journalistic misconduct by the *New York Times*. At some point between the initial controversies and Hannah-Jones's September 2020 media appearance, the newspaper quietly edited the text of the original 1619 Project on its website to remove a controversial passage designating 1619, rather than 1776, as the date of America's true founding. This deception marked a turning point in the trajectory of the larger project. It began as a flawed and one-sided look at American history that nonetheless spawned fruitful debate and discussion about slavery. After the edits and Hannah-Jones's public misrepresentation of them, the 1619 Project became almost exclusively political in nature. Its purpose shifted from initiating a historical discussion about slavery to covering up its own defects in a desperate bid to keep Hannah-Jones's political narrative intact.

The years that followed saw successive revisions of the original 1619 Project, first as an expanded book-length edition and then a documentary miniseries for the Hulu streaming service. If properly done, both products could have offered an opportunity to correct the factual and interpretive defects in the original series and invite a constructive discussion about the role of slavery in American history and culture. Instead, Hannah-Jones pressed ahead with additional cover-ups, exacerbating the shortcomings in the process.

A particular sore spot for Hannah-Jones emerged from criticism over the lack of expert oversight before the original 1619 Project went to print. Hannah-Jones's lead essay came under fire when one of its fact-checkers, historian Leslie M. Harris, revealed that the newspaper ignored her caution against

Preface to the Updated Edition | ix

portraying the American Revolution as a pro-slavery revolt against Britain. Desmond's essay had even more egregious problems, including a sloppy misreading of a key cited source and the author's general unfamiliarity with the complex and voluminous scholarly literature on the economics of slavery.

In response to these criticisms, Hannah-Jones sought cover behind the academic résumés of other writers for the project, including two academic historians who wrote essays about topics in 20th-century race relations. Neither historian wrote about the period when slavery actually existed or the crucial decades between the American founding in 1776 and the end of the Civil War in 1865. Instead, Hannah-Jones claimed this period for herself or shopped it out to journalists and nonexperts in other fields such as Desmond. When actual experts in this period scrutinized the original project's claims, they easily identified basic factual and interpretive errors that should have been noticed in the editing process. Most of the 1619 Project's difficulties originated with Hannah-Jones's failure to conduct basic peer review in the areas of the project's most controversial claims.

The book-length expansion of the 1619 Project published in early 2022 sought to paper over this problem by revising the existing essays to incorporate footnotes and by adding new chapters on adjacent themes from additional writers. The book edition expanded the series from 12 to 18 chapters and added several smaller vignettes on related topics. Although nonexperts still make up the majority of the authors, Hannah-Jones appears to have selected the new contributors with an eye toward bolstering the scholarly credibility of the original essays. At the same time, Hannah-Jones and Desmond made only minimal efforts to address the problems with their original essays. Both added footnote citations to their contributions, albeit almost entirely consisting of cherry-picked works from heterodox elements of the secondary historical literature that narrowly align with the two authors' political arguments. Neither endeavored to survey the broader scholarly landscape or answer the challenges published in response to the original 1619 Project. Instead, both doubled down on their original errors and augmented them with new mistakes from the fringes of academic writing, including adding an overt Marxist spin to their economic interpretations of slavery.

The more recent Hulu docuseries continues this descent into political advocacy, augmented by the tools of visual media and a high-dollar production budget. Again, Hannah-Jones leans into the same errors as the original series by augmenting them with anachronistic details and misleading filming locales. The final episode concludes with a tendentiously argued case for slavery reparations. Once Hannah-Jones finally arrives at the question of how to pay for such a program, her answer relies on the economic crankery of Modern Monetary Theory and a wishful insistence that payment of reparations would neither break the federal budget nor trigger an inflationary spiral.

The curious feature, then, of the 1619 Project's subsequent reinventions and expansions is an accompanying decline in quality and scholarly rigor. Each new permutation of Hannah-Jones's work has veered more heavily into political advocacy, taking greater liberties with evidence in the process. By implication, the original 1619 Project from the August 2019 *New York Times* magazine is also its least defective iteration. Its editor and creator could benefit from retrospection on her own role in this sad state of affairs, including the lost opportunities to host a productive discussion of slavery's historical legacy and its implications for the present. But doing so would also require abandoning the partisan activism that has guided most of her decisions since the original 1619 Project's release.

Phillip W. Magness
September 2024

Preface

WHEN I FIRST weighed in upon the *New York Times*'s 1619 Project, I was struck by its conflicted messaging. Comprising an entire magazine feature and a sizable advertising budget, the newspaper's initiative conveyed a serious attempt to engage the public in an intellectual exchange about the history of slavery in the United States and its lingering harms to our social fabric. It also seemed to avoid the superficiality of many public history initiatives, which all too often reduce over 400 complex years of slavery's history and legacy to sweeping generalizations. Instead, the *Times* promised detailed thematic explorations of topics ranging from the first slave ship's arrival in Jamestown, Virginia, in 1619 to the politics of race in the present day.

At the same time, however, certain 1619 Project essayists infused this worthy line of inquiry with a heavy stream of ideological advocacy. *Times* reporter Nikole Hannah-Jones announced this political intention openly, pairing progressive activism with the initiative's stated educational purposes.

Signs of the blurred lines between scholarship and activism appeared in several, though not all, of its essays. A historical discussion about the Constitution's notoriously strained handling of slavery quickly drifted into a list of partisan grievances against the tax and health care policy views of congressional Republicans in the twenty-first century. Another potentially interesting inquiry into the history of how city planning historically intertwined with racial segregation ended with a harangue against suburban Atlanta voters for declining to fund an expensive and ineffectual light-rail transit project at the ballot box. Hannah-Jones's own introductory essay presented a provocative conceptual reframing of American history around slavery, hence 1619 rather than 1776 as its titular origin date, albeit with an almost-singular mind toward advocating for a slavery-reparations program in the present.

Enlisting history for political editorializing is a time-honored habit of commentators across the political spectrum, so in a sense the 1619 Project's indulgences in the same were unexceptional. The *Times's* branding, however, exhibited a schizophrenia of purposes.

Hannah-Jones's own public comments pivoted between touting her work as the culmination of rigorous historical scholarship and an exercise in advocacy journalism—seemingly as the occasion demanded. The 1619 Project, it seemed, could serve as both an enduring long-term curriculum for high school and college classrooms and an activist manual for the 2020 campaign season. Unfortunately the blending of these two competing aims usually results in the sacrifice of scholarly standards in the service of the ideological objective—not by design, but by necessary implication of needing to reconcile the irreducible complexities of the past to a more simplistic political narrative.

This tendency finds its most visible display in the 1619 Project contribution that first caught my attention, Matthew Desmond's essay on the relationship between slavery and modern American capitalism. Having explored this topic extensively in my own scholarly work on economic and intellectual history, I was immediately struck by the shallow one-sidedness of Desmond's argument.

Among economic historians, few subjects are more heavily scrutinized than the operations of the antebellum slave economy. The existent literature dates back half a century and encompasses hundreds of works from across the ideological spectrum, each employing empirical data to better understand the profitability, efficiency, and state sanction of the plantation system. Curiously, Desmond's article evinced no awareness of the scholarly study of slavery beyond a narrow coterie of post-2010 historical works going by the moniker of the "New History of Capitalism" (NHC).

Although it has yielded modestly interesting archival insights about plantation operations, the NHC school of slavery scholarship also suffers from a notorious ideological and methodological insularity—the subject of a 2017 historiographical essay that I wrote for another book and that is adapted for the present volume. As that chapter documents, two defining characteristics of the NHC literature are (1) its recurring, and at times even inept, misuse of economic data to make unsupported empirical claims, and (2) its heavily anticapitalist political perspective. While both attributes have earned the NHC severe criticism among historians and economic historians of slavery from outside its ranks, the group has thus far taken few steps to reconcile its shortcomings with a broader scholarly literature that often belies the main NHC contentions. It therefore came as a surprise to find that Desmond had relied almost exclusively on contested claims from the NHC literature to build his argument, albeit without any hint of the associated contestation.

To this end, he casually repeated an erroneous NHC claim about the cause of cotton productivity growth in the early 19th century and further misrepresented its historical evidence to suggest an unsupported origin story for modern business practices in the accounting books of 19th-century plantations. The resulting argument advanced a specious link between slavery in the 19th century and capitalism today. Lurking beneath it all was a long list of Desmond's own modern progressive political causes—economic inequality, financial reforms after the 2007–8 financial crisis, and a general disdain for deregulation and free market thought. In short, Desmond was weaponizing the history of slavery to attack modern capitalism.

I entered the fray of the 1619 Project debate in its first week, with a series of articles scrutinizing Desmond's narrative and contextualizing them within what Friedrich A. Hayek dubbed the "anti-capitalist" tradition in intellectual life. From there I joined a broader discussion involving dozens of historians, economists, and other scholars that began to scrutinize other historical claims in the project, particularly Hannah-Jones's attempts to recast the American Revolution as being primarily motivated by the preservation of slavery.

Not all 1619 Project criticisms hit their mark though, and in the course of the ensuing months I broke from several of the other historian critics over the *Times*'s depiction of Abraham Lincoln. Hannah-Jones pointed out the sixteenth president's recurring interest in colonizing freed slaves abroad after emancipating them, mainly to call attention to Lincoln's complex and sometimes neglected beliefs about race in a post-slavery society. This earned her the animosity of a group of historian critics on both the political left and right, including accusations of unfairly disparaging Lincoln. Having devoted a significant amount of my own scholarly work to Lincoln's presidency, I weighed in on the arguments as presented, showing that the 1619 Project's assessment was in closer line with historical evidence that these critics neglected to consider. The essays are presented herein, and they place me in the curious position of being one of the only 1619 Project critics to also come to its defense on one of the major points of contention.

In assembling these essays, I make no claim of resolving what continues to be a vibrant and ongoing discussion. Neither should my work be viewed as the final arbiter of historical accuracy, though I do evaluate a number of factual and interpretive claims made by the project's authors. Rather, the aim is to provide an accessible resource for readers wishing to navigate the scholarly disputes, offering my own interpretive take on claims pertaining to areas of history in which I have worked.

Phillip W. Magness
March 2020

I

How the 1619 Project Rehabilitates the "King Cotton" Thesis

This essay, originally written for National Review, *examines the 1619 Project's heavy reliance on the New History of Capitalism (NHC) literature. A recurring theme of this literature is the unwitting rehabilitation of the "King Cotton" thesis—the notion that cotton occupied a commanding place in the 19th-century global economy, and as such the economic engines of the world were claimed to depend on plantation slavery. Confederate secessionists invented "King Cotton" as part of a pro-slavery propaganda campaign around the eve of the Civil War as an attempt to lure foreign allies to their cause.*

The war itself disproved the "King Cotton" premise, as foreign powers simply turned elsewhere for their cotton supply and the Confederacy collapsed in economic isolation from the world. While most economic historians since that time have recognized the error of logic behind the "King Cotton" theory, the recent NHC literature has revived it—minus the Confederates' slavery defenses—in an attempt to restore cotton to a historically untenable place as the centerpiece of 19th-century capitalism.

"I SAY THAT cotton is king, and that he waves his scepter not only over these 33 states, but over the island of Great Britain and over continental Europe!" So thundered Senator Louis T. Wigfall of Texas in December 1860, as an intended warning to those who doubted the economic viability of secessionism. Like many Southerners, Wigfall subscribed to the "King Cotton" thesis: the belief that slave-produced cotton commanded a controlling position over the American economy and indeed the world's commercial engines. Developed in the 1850s by political economist David Christy and championed by the radical pro-slavery politician James Henry Hammond, that argument was to be the nascent Confederacy's trump card—an engine of global wealth in which all other economic activities were intertwined. Indeed, no nation would dare make war upon plantation slavery, for if the South suspended its production, in the words of Hammond, "we could bring the whole world to our feet."

The strategy failed. The secessionists effectively self-embargoed what remained of their export crop in the wake of the war's physical destruction and the Union's blockade, and attempts to draw the European powers into the war on the Confederacy's behalf were unsuccessful. King Cotton, in practice, proved nothing more than part self-delusion and part racist propaganda to rationalize the supposed economic necessity of chattel slavery. Modern empirical analysis has similarly debunked its claims: As Harvard economist Nathan Nunn has demonstrated, a strong negative relationship exists between the historical existence of slavery in a county or state and its level of income, persisting to the present day.[1]

Yet despite its historical untenability, the economic reasoning behind "King Cotton" has undergone a surprising—perhaps unwitting—rehabilitation through a modern genre of scholarly works known as the New History of Capitalism (NHC). While NHC historians reject the pro-slavery thrust of Wigfall and Hammond's bluster, they recast slave-produced cotton as "not just as an integral part of American capitalism, but . . . its very essence," to quote Harvard's Sven Beckert. Cornell historian Ed Baptist goes even further, describing slavery as the indispensable causal driver behind America's wealth today. Cotton production, he contends, was "absolutely necessary" for the Western world to break the "10,000-year Malthusian cycle of agriculture."

And this same NHC literature provides the scholarly foundation of the ballyhooed *New York Times*'s 1619 Project—specifically, its foray into the economics of slavery. Guided by this rehabilitated version of King Cotton, Princeton sociologist Matthew Desmond enlists the horrors of the plantation system to launch a blistering attack on modern American capitalism.

Desmond projects slavery's legacy onto a litany of tropes about rising inequality, the decline of labor-union power, environmental destruction, and the 2008 financial crisis. The intended message is clear: modern capitalism carries with it the stain of slavery, and its putative excesses are proof of its continued brutality. It follows that only by abandoning the free market and embracing political redistribution will we ever atone for this tainted inheritance.

It's not just the *New York Times* that uses NHC scholarship to distort the economic history of the U.S. At a congressional hearing earlier this summer, journalist Ta-Nehisi Coates enlisted another of Baptist's claims to argue for reparations. "By 1836 more than $600 million, almost half of the economic activity in the United States, derived directly or indirectly from the cotton produced by the million-odd slaves," Coates said.

This stunning statistic quickly became one of the most memorable sound bites of the occasion. It is also unambiguously false—the result of Baptist double- and triple-counting intermediate transactions from cotton production to artificially increase its economic share.[2] Through an elementary accounting error, Baptist had inflated the actual size of the cotton sector by almost tenfold. At approximately 5 to 6 percent of the antebellum economy, cotton did indeed constitute a major output, roughly comparable in size to the northern-dominated railroad sector. It was not, however, the commercial monarch of either Confederate fantasy or Baptist's revisionism.

Dubious statistical claims and shoddy research practices are alarmingly common in the broader NHC literature. Those who rely on it repeat these mistakes. In the 1619 Project, Desmond uses another of Baptist's statistics to attribute a 400 percent increase in the daily yield of cotton-picking between 1800 and 1860 to the systematization of whipping and torture as a means of increasing production. This "calibrated torture" thesis forms the central claim of Baptist's 2014 book, *The Half Has Never Been Told*, purporting to show that slave-based production was a capitalistic enterprise at its core. Furthermore, Baptist claims that modern industrial-management techniques (the recording of daily outputs, the comparative tracking of employee productivity, the keeping of double-entry accounting books) take a page from the most evil chapter of American history.

Yet again, Baptist's thesis is built on misinterpreted evidence—or perhaps intentional deception. He bases his argument on the empirical work of economists Alan Olmstead and Paul Rhode, who assembled decades of plantation records to study the growth in cotton-crop yields before the Civil War. Olmstead and Rhode discovered the same 400 percent increase in cotton-picking rates yet found a completely different cause: yields grew primarily as a result of technological improvements to the crop from cross-breeding different strains of cotton seed.

Olmstead and Rhode published a stinging rebuke of Baptist's work, showing empirically that cotton-picking yields tended to follow daily variations across the crop season, not Baptist's posited use of a torture-enforced quota system.[3] In addition to his faulty GDP statistics, they showed that Baptist severely overstated the amount of wealth tied up in slavery. "The upshot," they note, "is that slaves represented an important share of U.S. wealth but not nearly as great as Baptist claimed."

They also uncovered evidence of Baptist massaging the details of primary-source accounts such as slave narratives to bolster his thesis. This included adding words to slave testimonies and blending passages from disparate sources to change their meaning. These suspicious edits make accounts of the treatment of slaves appear more similar to modern-day managerial tactics.

The economists do not contest or downplay the violent reality of plantation life, acknowledging openly that the widespread "use of violence or the threat of violence increased slave output." But they document several instances of Baptist playing fast and loose with the evidence, either to exaggerate the resemblance of chattel slavery to modern managerial practices or to inflate the size of the plantation system and treat it as the single dominant economic force in antebellum America.

Curiously, participants of the 1619 Project evince little awareness of the deep historical deficiencies in Baptist's work or of similar problems among the other NHC scholars on whom they rest their case. When I asked Nikole Hannah-Jones, the project's editor, about its repetition of erroneous and contested economic claims, she said, "Economists dispute a few of Baptist's calculations but not the book itself nor its thesis."[4]

Really? Contrast that with Olmstead's concluding assessment: "Edward Baptist's study of capitalism and slavery is flawed beyond repair."[5] Or Wellesley economist Eric Hilt's review essay, in which he identifies "specious arguments and failures of analytical reasoning" in the NHC literature and chastises the genre for the way its "neglect of insights from economic history often weakens its analysis and undermines its credibility as social criticism."[6] Or the observation by Stanley Engerman, who in his co-authored work *Time on the Cross* defined the modern field on the economics of slavery, that Baptist does not meaningfully engage with "the last decades of works concerning economic aspects of the slave economy," many of which cut directly against his conclusions.[7] Indeed, much of the self-asserted novelty of the NHC historians seems to reflect their own unfamiliarity with the economic literature on the same subject. And Baptist, to his discredit, has generally declined to answer the substantive criticisms of his work, even as his errors spread to wider audiences via the press.

Like the original "King Cotton" thesis, the NHC suffers from its own ideological disposition. Though one sought to prop up slavery in its own day and the other condemns it historically, both build their evidence by working backward from the preexisting conclusion of its economic vitality. Both then advance the simply false assertion that this economic vitality was the driving engine of the antebellum economy.

The thrust of these exaggerations is to recast slavery as a distinctly capitalistic enterprise, which, in turn, services the 1619 Project's political message. The worthy historical task of documenting the horrors of American slavery has been cynically repurposed into an ideological attack on free-market capitalism. But in a curious final twist, the "King Cotton" theorists of old would have likely balked at the decision by their latter-day inheritors to label plantation slavery a capitalistic enterprise. To the original pro-slavery theorists, the very free-market theories that Baptist and the *New York Times* indict were an existential threat. The philosophical doctrines we now know as capitalism were "tainted with abolition, and at war with our institutions," to quote an 1857 tract by leading pro-slavery theorist George Fitzhugh. For slavery to survive this attack, he said, the South must "throw Adam Smith, Say, Ricardo & Co., in the fire."[8]

Insofar as the 1619 Project seeks to teach American society about the horrific historical legacy of slavery, it is no small irony that a significant part of the project borrows from a historical literature that apparently envisions a similar future for Adam Smith's heirs.

2

The Anti-Capitalist Ideology of Slavery

In this essay, I examine the first of many oversights in Matthew Desmond's 1619 Project essay, in which he asserts that American capitalism is infused with the brutality of the slave system. Briefly, his account completely neglects the role of intellectual history in defining and interpreting capitalism. Upon examining this history, two trends emerge.

First, the originators of what we now refer to as "capitalism"— the free market liberal tradition that passed from Adam Smith to the laissez-faire and free trade traditions of Richard Cobden and Frederic Bastiat—had a directly adversarial view of slavery. Economists and political writers in this tradition heavily overlapped with the contemporary abolitionist movement and tended to view slavery as both morally and economically repulsive.

Second, pro-slavery theorists of this same period also held capitalism in contempt—and especially its laissez-faire iteration. I document this pronounced hostility to capitalism in the work of George Fitzhugh, the leading pro-slavery theorist of the late antebellum period. For academics such as Desmond who wish to forge a conceptual alliance between slavery and capitalism, this historical record of capitalism's proponents and adversaries remains a substantial and unaccounted obstacle.

WHAT IS CAPITALISM'S view toward slavery? It seems like a crazy question, but not so much actually, not in these times. So let us begin with the opening line of the first chapter of George Fitzhugh's *Sociology for the South*, first published in 1854:[1]

> Political economy is the science of free society. Its theory and its history alike establish this position. Its fundamental maxim Laissez-faire and "Pas trop gouverner," are at war with all kinds of slavery, for they in fact assert that individuals and peoples prosper most when governed least.

Fitzhugh's point was to inveigh against economic freedom and in defense of slavery. His radical tract sought to make out an elaborate ideological case for slave labor and indeed all aspects of social ordering. Such a system, he announced, would resolve the posited state of perpetual conflict between labor and the owners of capital by supplanting it with the paternalistic hierarchy of slavery—a model he advocated not only for the plantations of the South but also for adaptation to the factories of the Northeast.

In total, Fitzhugh presented a horrifying vision of a national society reordered around the principle of chattel slavery. And as his introductory remarks announced, attainment of that society required the defeat of its remaining obstacle, the free market.

Although his theories are rightly rejected today, the Virginia-born Fitzhugh attained national prominence in the late antebellum period as one of the most widely read defenders of a slave-based economy. Charles Sumner called him a "leading writer among Slave-masters," and his regular contributions to the pro-South magazine *De Bow's Review* gained him a national readership in the 1850s.

In 1855 Fitzhugh embarked on a publicity tour of the Northeast, jousting with abolitionist Wendell Phillips in a series of back-to-back lectures on the slavery question. By 1861, he had added his voice to the cause of Southern secessionism and began mapping out an elaborate slave-based industrialization policy for the Confederacy's wartime economy.[2]

Fitzhugh was also an avowed anti-capitalist. Slavery's greatest threat came from the free market economic doctrines of Europe, which were "tainted with abolition, and at war with our institutions." According to him, the South's survival required "throw[ing] Adam Smith, Say, Ricardo & Co., in the fire."

Such rhetoric presents an under-acknowledged conundrum for modern historians. In contemporary academia it has become trendy to depict plantation slavery as an integral component of American capitalism.

A new multipart feature series in the *New York Times* advances this thesis, depicting modern free market capitalism as an inherently "racist" institution and a direct lineal descendant of plantation slavery, still exhibiting the brutality of that system.[3] This characterization draws heavily from the so-called "New History of Capitalism" (NHC)—a genre of historical writing that swept through the academy in the last decade and that aggressively promotes the thesis that free market capitalism and slavery are inextricably linked.

Many leading examples of NHC scholarship in the academy today are plagued by shoddy economic analysis and documented misuse of historical evidence.[4] These works often present historically implausible arguments, such as the notion that modern double-entry accounting emerged from plantation ledger books (the practice actually traces to the banking economies of Renaissance Italy), or that its use by slave owners is distinctively capitalistic (even the Soviets employed modern accounting practices, despite attempting to centrally plan their entire economy). Indeed, it was NHC historian Ed Baptist who produced an unambiguously false statistic purporting to show that cotton production accounted for a full half of the antebellum American economy (when in actual fact it comprised about 5 percent of GDP).[5]

Despite the deep empirical and historical deficiencies of this literature, NHC arguments are still widely enlisted not only as historical analysis of slavery's economics but as an ideological attack on modern capitalism itself. If capitalism is historically tainted by its links to slavery, they reason, then the effects of slavery's stain persist in modern American capitalism today. In its most extreme iterations, these same historians then advocate a political reordering of the American economy to remove that stain. In other words, to reconcile our society to its history and atone for the sins of slavery, we must abandon what remains of American capitalism.

The NHC literature's use of the term "capitalism" is plagued by its own definitional fluidity, which, at times, encompasses everything from laissez-faire non-intervention to protectionist mercantilism to state-ordered central planning. Most economic historians take care to differentiate between the features of these widely varying systems; however, the NHC literature has adopted a habit of simply relabeling everything as "capitalism." A command-and-control wartime industrial policy thus becomes "war capitalism," while a slave-oriented mercantilist regime of protective tariffs and industrial subsidies becomes "racial slave capitalism," and so forth.

When brandished in modern politics, it quickly becomes clear that the same scholars have only one "capitalism" in mind. The NHC genre's own economic inclinations veer unambiguously in a leftward direction, suggesting their real ire is toward the classical liberal free market variety of capitalism. Wealth redistribution, the nationalization of health care and other entire economic sectors, socialistic central planning of industries around labor activism, and even a plethora of climate change policies thereby become necessary acts of "social justice" to correct for capitalism's supposed slavery-infused legacy.

We therefore arrive at the curious position wherein "atonement" for slavery, as presented by the NHC historians, involves politically repudiating the same free market doctrines that Fitzhugh deemed the greatest danger to slavery itself in the decade before the Civil War.

Returning to Fitzhugh's defense of slavery, we find deep similarities to anti-capitalist rhetoric today. The economic doctrines of laissez-faire, he wrote in 1857, foster "a system of unmitigated selfishness."[6] They subject nominally free labor to the "despotism of capital" wherein the capitalist class extracts an "exploitation of skill" from wage laborers, as found in the difference between the value of what they create and the much lower compensation they receive.

As Fitzhugh argued, by way of the example of a wealthy acquaintance who had "ceased work" and lived off of his fortune, the capitalist's "capital was but the accumulation of the results of their labor; for common labor creates all capital." He then succinctly explained the result by noting "the capitalist, living on his income, gives nothing to his subjects. He lives by mere exploitation." As Fitzhugh continued:

> It is the interest of the capitalist and the skillful to allow free laborers the least possible portion of the fruits of their own labor; for all capital is created by labor, and the smaller the allowance of the free laborer, the greater the gains of his employer. To treat free laborers badly and unfairly, is universally inculcated as a moral duty, and the selfishness of man's nature prompts him to the most rigorous performance of this cannibalish duty. We appeal

to political economy; the ethical, social, political and economic philosophy of free society, to prove the truth of our doctrines. As an ethical and social guide, that philosophy teaches, that social, individual and national competition, is a moral duty, and we have attempted to prove all competition is but the effort to enslave others, without being encumbered with their support.

The difference between the value of the laborer's product and this substantially lower wage, Fitzhugh explained, provided a measure of the exploited share of his work.

If this line of reasoning sounds familiar, it is due to a very real parallel between Fitzhugh's formulation of the capital–labor relationship and that of another famous contemporary. Fitzhugh had effectively worked out the Marxian theory of "surplus value" over a decade before the publication of Marx's own *Capital* (1867), and derived it from the same sweeping indictment of the free-labor capitalism.

The two thinkers would only diverge in their next steps, the prescriptive solution. Whereas Marx rejected chattel slavery and extrapolated a long historical march to an eventual socialist reordering through revolutionary upheaval, Fitzhugh saw a readily available alternative. "Slavery is a form, and the very best form, of socialism," he explained. Wage labor, he predicted, would be forever insufficient to meet the needs of the laborer due to deprivation of his products from his skill. Slavery, to Fitzhugh's convenience, could step in and fill the gap through the paternalistic provision of necessities for the enslaved, allegedly removing the "greed" of wage exploitation from the process.

Since slaves became the charge of the slave master and were placed under his care for food and shelter, Fitzhugh reasoned that "slaves consume more of the results of their own labor than laborers at the North." Plantation slavery, according to this contorted line of thinking, thereby mitigated the "exploitation" of wage labor capitalism and returned a greater portion of the posited surplus value. In the Marxian counterpart, a socialist state fulfills a similar function.

Fitzhugh's eccentric extrapolation from what are essentially Marxian doctrines has the effect of turning Marx's own untenable "solution" to capital ownership on its head. But the two thinkers unite in their grievances: a shared enmity toward market capitalism, and a desire to cast free market allocation of resources aside through coercive social reordering to achieve their respective ideal societies—mass enslavement or global communism.

These similarities between Fitzhugh and socialism, and indeed the aggressive anti-capitalist rhetoric of pro-slavery ideology, are seldom examined in the NHC literature. In its quest to politically tar modern capitalism with the horrors of slavery, these historians have adopted a practice of evidentiary negligence that conveniently excludes the explicit anti-capitalist ideological tenets of the very same slave system that they rebrand as a foundation of the modern capitalist economy.

Fitzhugh was not alone in adopting and adapting anti-capitalist ideology to the defense of slavery. Indeed, he heavily extrapolated it from Thomas Carlyle's own racist attacks upon the "dismal science" of economics on account of its close historical ties to abolitionism.[7] That these pro-slavery thinkers found a parallel rationale in socialism and deployed it to attack a common enemy of free markets, irrespective of their otherwise-divergent claims, is indicative of a shared illiberalism between the two. In practice, unfortunately, the immiserating historical records of each reveal that the only remaining distinction between their political outcomes consists of the choice between the slavery of the plantation and the slavery of the gulag.

3

How Capitalist-Abolitionists Fought Slavery

This article tells the little-known story of Lewis Tappan, a wealthy New York abolitionist who financed several of the most important publications and institutions in the American anti-slavery movement. Tappan's philanthropy caused an immense slaveholder backlash against his business interests. Rather than surrender to insolvency and ruin, he found a way to use free market institutions to circumvent a slaveholder boycott and slaveholder attempts to defraud his company.

RUNNING AFOUL OF slave-owning political interests almost destroyed brothers Lewis and Arthur Tappan, the wealthy owners of a prominent New York mercantile import business. On July 9, 1834, a pro-slavery mob gathered at New York City's Chatham Street Chapel with the intention of breaking up an abolitionist sermon.

Among their many grievances, the protesters were incensed at an incident some weeks earlier in which Arthur invited Rev. Samuel Cornish, an African-American abolitionist and cofounder of the American Anti-Slavery Society, into his family pew for Sunday service. The gesture served as a powerful symbolic call for the racial integration of religious worship at the chapel. It also made the Tappan brothers—already well-known as a philanthropic force behind the abolitionist movement—the target of sensationalist conspiracy theorizing that spread to newspapers across the country and accused the devoutly Christian and pacifist brothers of fomenting a slave revolt.

Congregants caught wind of threats to forcibly disrupt their gathering and fled for their own safety. Still seeking a fight, the mob descended upon

Lewis Tappan's nearby home, tossing its furniture into a fire on the street and successfully driving away an attempt by the New York police to quell the riot. For the next two days, breakaway mobs searched the city for the Tappan brothers, ransacking the homes of both white abolitionists and leaders of New York's free black community in the process. The same mobs attacked African-Americans on the streets at random and held crude racist political demonstrations in front of churches and businesses they deemed friendly to the abolitionist cause.

The Tappan brothers managed to escape relatively unscathed as the mayor stationed an armed militia to guard their storefront and drive away rioters. National news of the Chatham Incident, or "Tappan Riots" as they came to be called, carried other repercussions. It made the firm of Arthur Tappan & Co. into the target of a slave owner–instigated boycott that preyed upon public racism to drive away its customer base.

The mob targeting of the Tappans proved to be a watershed moment in the crusade to end slavery. William Lloyd Garrison's coverage of the riots demonstrated that slavery's defenders were willing to incite political violence in order to silence their critics. The episode also converted New York journalist William Leggett to the cause of abolition, which he then explicitly linked to a philosophy of laissez-faire capitalism and free trade.[1]

It also took a heavy toll on the Tappans' company. If the pro-slavery mob could not physically drive them from their New York business, it would destroy them nationally through a vilification campaign and economic targeting. Newspapers across the South demonized the brothers as the face of not only abolitionism but racial intermarriage, black political rights, and violent slave revolts. Groups of slave owners in New Orleans and Charleston even pledged a bounty on Arthur Tappan's head. A poster advertising a "$20,000 Reward for Tappan," for example, appears prominently in an 1835 depiction of slave owners ransacking a post office to intercept copies of William Lloyd Garrison's *The Liberator*.[2]

By 1837, the combined loss of business from the boycott and the descent of the American economy into a deep financial depression left the brothers owing more than $1 million to creditors. The decline represented a nearly complete reversal in fortunes for a firm previously known for its conservative bookkeeping and heavy reliance on cash transactions to limit its liabilities

ATTACK ON THE POST OFFICE, CHARLESTON, S.C.

from customers who reneged on their payment obligations. Arthur Tappan & Co. finally closed shop.

Lewis Tappan, who often spoke of his business as a moral charge and who directed its proceeds in healthier times to a variety of abolitionist newspapers, was not yet ready to concede the fight to an orchestrated campaign of financial ruination. At his darkest moment, he came up with a brilliant plan that not only reversed his fortunes but also revolutionized the American financial industry.

Drawing on the experience of the boycott, Lewis recognized a systemic fault in the existing practices for business transactions carried out on credit. To fight back against a slave owner–incited boycott that undermined their cash purchases, the Tappans would reconstitute their business model around their existing network of connections in the abolitionist movement by offering credit transactions to trusted friends and associates. Establishing that trust, however, remained an obstacle, particularly if they ever hoped to expand this service beyond their own personal associations.

The complexities of the global import market and a growing customer base, spread across the nation's rapidly expanding geography, made the issuance of credit into an economic challenge. What was once a simple relationship between a shopkeeper and customers who were known to Lewis and who usually resided in his neighborhood now became a persistent information problem. With expanded markets, businesses could no longer afford to rely upon personal knowledge and reputation when vetting potential customers. A firm had to either insist upon payment up front or assume the risk that a customer would abscond with goods purchased on credit. The only available solutions were to pay for individual background checks on potential clients before extending them credit—an expensive and unwieldy undertaking for all but the largest of firms—or absorb the loss if a customer reneged on repayment.

Lewis Tappan devised an innovative solution to this problem by creating a service to independently track and validate the credit-worthiness of potential clients. In 1841 he founded the New York Mercantile Agency, the first modern credit-reporting firm in the United States. The new company offered a subscription-based service that collected and maintained a list of the credit-worthiness ratings of private businesses across New York City and, eventually, the country.

Reaching into his network of abolitionist connections and known clients from his old firm, Tappan was then able to assemble a network of credit investigators and attorneys who used local knowledge to assemble reports about outstanding debts, repayment rates, and defaults among the businesses in their cities and towns. A rating could then be provided to subscribers of the service, allowing them to reliably evaluate the risk of doing business with firms located thousands of miles away. The information problem at the root of previously complex credit arrangements could be mitigated through a market service that independently verified business reputations and conveyed their creditworthiness over long distances through simple consultation of a low-cost subscription paper.

Lewis Tappan's innovation revolutionized the American finance industry. The direct successor to his Mercantile Agency still exists today as Dun & Bradstreet, and his idea of an independent credit-reporting entity became the standard verification instrument of modern business lending and investment practices. The information it provided as an external and accessible measure of reputation, in turn, allowed for reliable and regular transactions to occur over long distances, thereby helping to ignite an unprecedented expansion of access to markets and goods across the nation.

The origins of Tappan's innovation remain a neglected feature in the history of American capitalism. A succinct account of the Mercantile Agency's history may be found in an article by historians Brian Grinder and Dan Cooper for the Museum of American Finance.[3] For a longer discussion, I recommend Roy A. Foulke's 1941 text *The Sinews of American Commerce,* which details its abolitionist origins.[4]

Their fortunes renewed, the Tappan brothers remained devoted benefactors of the abolitionist cause. After the Fugitive Slave Act of 1850 strengthened federal government efforts to recapture African-Americans in the North and return them to slavery, the brothers set up a network of lawyers to mount legal challenges to the renditions and, where possible, funneled money to support the Underground Railroad. Lewis also subsidized Lysander Spooner's book *The Unconstitutionality of Slavery* and financed the printing of his abolitionist pamphlets.[5]

Interest in the history of American capitalism is on the rise, although curiously this line of study is being advanced for anti-capitalistic ideological reasons as may be found in the *New York Times*'s new 1619 Project on American slavery. Much of the associated academic literature, including sources used by the *Times,* relies on empirically shoddy and politicized lines of research that several leading economic historians have conclusively refuted.[6]

In eschewing factual analysis for political narratives, the scholars and journalists involved in the 1619 Project appear to be far more interested in weaponizing the history of slavery with biased and even fabricated claims for the purpose of discrediting capitalism and free markets in the present day. They neglect the historical antagonism that existed between slave owners and free market capitalism, including a leading slavery defender who declared that capitalism was "at war with all kinds of slavery."[7]

It is therefore no small irony that one of the most important innovations in American financial history—the development of a reliable and replicable credit-reporting mechanism—owes its existence to a leading capitalist benefactor of the American anti-slavery movement. That innovation emerged as a tool for abolitionist business owners to escape violent harassment by racist mobs and coordinated economic targeting by plantation owners who sought to destroy the viability of their businesses. Lewis Tappan illustrated through his personal struggle and his economic entrepreneurship that American capitalism was, indeed, at war with slavery.

4

The Statistical Errors of the Reparations Agenda

This article predates the 1619 Project by a few months, but touches directly on a faulty statistical claim that informs the broader New History of Capitalism (NHC) literature on which the Times *relies. A widely repeated passage from a book by NHC historian Edward Baptist incorrectly asserts that slave-produced cotton accounted for almost half of the antebellum economy's gross domestic product (GDP). As I investigate and discuss, Baptist's claim is based on an elementary misunderstanding of how GDP is calculated that causes him to double- and triple-count several intermediate steps of cotton production. The actual share of antebellum GDP accounted for by cotton is closer to 5 percent.*

JOURNALIST AND POLITICAL commentator Ta-Nehisi Coates drew attention to the political cause of slavery reparations during a heavily publicized congressional hearing this week.[1] While commentators on both sides of the issue agree that his case was eloquently argued, one of its central claims rested on faulty economic data.

Specifically, Coates contends that the case for reparations comes from the economic measurement of the antebellum slave economy in the United States. He testified, "By 1836 more than $600 million, almost half of the economic activity in the United States, derived directly or indirectly from the cotton produced by the million-odd slaves."

This stunning statistical claim was widely repeated in commentary on the hearing. It is, however, unambiguously false.

Coates's numbers come from Cornell University historian Ed Baptist's 2014 book *The Half Has Never Been Told*.[2] In a key passage in the book, Baptist purports to add up the total value of economic activity that derived from cotton production, which at $77 million made up about 5 percent of the estimated gross domestic product (GDP) of the United States in 1836. Baptist then committed a fundamental accounting error. He proceeded to double and even triple count intermediate transactions involved in cotton production—things like land purchases for plantations, tools used for cotton production, transportation, insurance, and credit instruments used in each. Eventually that $77 million became $600 million in Baptist's accounting, or almost half of the entire antebellum economy of the United States.

There's a crucial problem with Baptist's approach. The calculation of GDP, the main formulation of national accounts and a representation of the dollar amount of economic activity in a country in a given year, only incorporates the value of final goods and services produced. The rationale for doing so comes from accounting, as the price of the final good already incorporates intermediate transactions that go into its production and distribution. Baptist's numbers are not only wrong—they reflect a basic unfamiliarity with the meaning and definition of GDP.

When *The Half Has Never Been Told* first appeared in print, economists immediately picked up on the error. Bradley Hansen of Mary Washington University kicked off the scrutiny by posting a thorough dissection of Baptist's errors on his personal blog.[3] Economic historians Alan Olmstead and Paul Rhode, of UC Davis and the University of Michigan respectively, chimed in with a devastating critique of Baptist's empirics, observing that a continuation of his "faulty methodology by summing the 'roles' of cotton with a few other primary products" would yield an amount that "easily exceed[ed] 100 percent of GDP" in the antebellum United States—an economic impossibility.[4]

Stanley Engerman, perhaps the foremost living expert on the economics of slavery, weighed in next:[5]

> Baptist's economic analysis, intended to demonstrate the essential role of the slave-grown cotton economy for Northern economic growth, is weakened by some variants of double- and triple-counting and some confusion of assets and income flows. To go from a value of the Southern cotton crop in 1836 of "about 5

percent of that entire gross domestic product," to "almost half of the economic activity of the United States in 1836" (pp 312–22) requires his calculation to resemble the great effects claimed by an NFL club when trying to convince city taxpayers that they should provide the money to build a new stadium because of all the stadium's presumed primary and secondary effects.

The main takeaways are that (1) the actual percentage of GDP derived from slavery is measured from final goods and services that involved slave-based production, and (2) Ed Baptist clearly did not understand what he was doing when he calculated his statistic. Cotton was by far the biggest item on the list of final goods and services, and, while its output varied year by year, it is probably reasonable to place slave-based goods in the mid to high single digits, not the 50 percent claim that Coates repeated.

Unfortunately, historians who work on the "New History of Capitalism"—a school of historiography that emerged after the financial crisis of 2007–8 and that purports to study the relationship between slavery and capitalism—have proven remarkably ill-suited to grasping the fundamentals of GDP and other economic concepts.

Not to be outdone by Baptist's erroneous 50 percent estimate, Emory University historian Carol Anderson offered an even higher figure from the eve of the Civil War itself. According to Anderson, "80 percent of the nation's gross national product was tied to slavery" in 1860. Following Coates's testimony using Baptist's erroneous numbers for 1836, several historians began circulating this estimate from Anderson's 2016 book *White Rage* as evidence of the growing influence of slavery on American capitalism in the late antebellum period.[6]

Like Baptist's book, it too derives from a fundamentally erroneous understanding of national accounts. Anderson's footnote points to the late historian David Brion Davis's foreword to a 2010 book on abolitionism. Davis makes a very different claim, however, in noting that the total value of slaves on the eve of the Civil War was equal to 80 percent of a *single year's* gross national product (GNP).[7] Anderson appears to have misread Davis's data point and transformed it into a broader claim about slavery's share of the entire economy.

While this figure is admittedly astounding and signifies the vast amount of wealth tied up in Southern slavery, Anderson mistakes it for the recurring *yearly* value of slave-produced economic output. She therefore commits the basic economic error of confusing stocks—by definition, a one-time measurement—and flows, which are measured over time. As we've already seen from Baptist's example though, the actual percentage of GDP (or GNP) tied up in slavery was actually a small fraction of that amount.

Basic statistical errors of this type are a pervasive feature of the "New History of Capitalism" genre of scholarship—even to the point that they are now entering into the discourse over policy discussions, as Coates's widely touted testimony at the reparations hearing illustrates.

In each case, the historians' demonstrably wrong GDP and GNP numbers make for a shocking claim that appears to situate slave production at the very core of all American economic activity before the Civil War. This claim appears to confirm many of the ideological expectations of the same historians, who also evince a pronounced hostility to market capitalism throughout their work. Linking historical capitalism to slavery is more of a political exercise for the present day than a scholarly inquiry into the past, and in fact the most virulent defenders of slavery in the mid-19th century actually presented their cause as an expressly anti-capitalist venture.[8]

There is a great moral gravity to discussions of slavery, not only as a historical problem but also an institution with persistent and adverse legacies that remain with us. It is therefore a timely and ever-present subject of scholarly inquiry and discussion. Regardless of where one stands on the reparations debate or other causes in the modern political scene, academics owe the public an honest, accurate, and scientific assessment of slavery's history, including its economic dimensions. That assessment is harmed when the discussion forgoes scientific rigor or even basic statistical practices to rally around a mistaken number in support of misleading and grossly inaccurate conclusions about the nature of the antebellum economy. Baptist, Coates, and the other public figures who have repeated this faulty statistic have an obligation to correct their error.

5

Fact-Checking the 1619 Project and Its Critics

I wrote this essay as an extended assessment of the debate between the historian critics of the 1619 Project and the Times's *Jake Silverstein, following the simultaneous publication of each in the paper's letters section in December 2019. I evaluate each of the four contested claims and link to appropriate scholarly literature. Briefly, I find that (1) the historians have a stronger but not uncontested case on the role of slavery in the American Revolution, (2) the 1619 Project has a stronger argument on Abraham Lincoln, (3) the historians are correct to chastise the New History of Capitalism literature, and (4) the* Times *appears to have done an inadequate job at seeking scholarly guidance for the 1619 Project's sections on the American Revolution, slavery, and the Civil War, although it also did a much better job at externally vetting its claims on the 20th century and present day.*

THE NEW YORK TIMES'S 1619 Project entered a new phase of historical assessment when the paper published a scathing criticism by five well-known historians of the American Revolution and Civil War eras. The group included previous critics James McPherson, Gordon Wood, Victoria Bynum, and James Oakes, along with a new signature from Sean Wilentz. The newspaper's editor-in-chief, Jake Silverstein, then responded with a point-by-point rebuttal of the historians, defending the project.[1]

Each deserves to be taken seriously, as they form part of a larger debate on the merits of the 1619 Project as a work of history and its intended use in the K–12 classroom curriculum. While the project itself spans some four centuries, devoting substantial attention to racial discrimination against African-

Americans in the present day, the historians' criticism focuses almost entirely on the two articles that are most directly pertinent to their own areas of expertise. The first is the lengthy introductory essay by Nikole Hannah-Jones, the *Times* journalist who edited the project. The second is a contentious essay on the relationship between slavery and American capitalism by Princeton University sociologist Matthew Desmond.

How should readers assess the competing claims of each group, seeing as they appear to be at bitter odds? That question is subject to a multitude of interpretive issues raised by the project's stated political aims, as well as the historians' own objectives as eminent figures—some might say gatekeepers—in the academic end of the profession.

But the debate may also be scored on its many disputed factual claims. To advance that discussion, I accordingly offer an assessment for each of the main points of contention as raised by the historians' letter and Silverstein's response.

1. Was the American Revolution fought in defense of slavery?

One of the most hotly contested claims of the 1619 Project appears in its introductory essay by Nikole Hannah-Jones, who writes that "one of the primary reasons the colonists decided to declare their independence from Britain was because they wanted to protect the institution of slavery."

Hannah-Jones cites this claim to two historical events. The first is the 1772 British legal case of *Somerset v. Stewart*, which reasoned from English common law that a slave taken by his owner from the colonies to Great Britain could not be legally held against his will. England had never established slavery by positive law, therefore Somerset was free to go.

The second event she enlists is a late 1775 proclamation by Lord Dunmore, the colonial governor of Virginia, in which he offered freedom to slaves who would take up arms for the loyalist cause against the stirring rebellion.[2] The measure specified that it was "appertaining to Rebels" only, thereby exempting any slaves owned by loyalists.

Hannah-Jones argues that these two events revealed that British colonial rule presented an emerging threat to the continuation of slavery, thereby providing an impetus for slave-owning Americans to support independence. The

American Revolution, she contends, was motivated in large part to "ensure slavery would continue." The five historians vigorously dispute this claimed causality, indicating that it exaggerates the influence of these events vis-à-vis better known objects of colonial ire, as stated in the Declaration of Independence.

There is a kernel of truth in Hannah-Jones's interpretation of these events. Somerset's case is traditionally seen as the starting point of Britain's own struggle for emancipation, and Dunmore's proclamation certainly provoked the ire of slave owners in the southern colonies—although they were more likely to interpret it as an attempt to foment the threat of a slave revolt as a counter-revolutionary strategy than a sign that Britain itself would impose emancipation in the near future.

Curiously unmentioned in the dispute is a much clearer case of how the loyalist cause aligned itself with emancipation, albeit in a limited sense. As part of his evacuation of New York City in 1783, British commander Sir Guy Carleton secured the removal of over 3,000 slaves for resettlement in Nova Scotia. This action liberated more than ten times as many slaves as Dunmore's proclamation, the earlier measure having been offered as part of an increasingly desperate bid to retain power long after colonial opinion turned against him. Carleton's removal also became a source of recurring tensions for U.S.–British relations after the war's settlement. Alexander Hamilton, representing New York, even presented a resolution before the Confederation Congress demanding the return of this human "property" to their former owners.[3]

That much noted, Hannah-Jones's argument must be assessed against the broader context of British emancipation. It is here that the five historians gain the stronger case. First, despite both its high symbolic importance and later use as a case precedent, the *Somerset* ruling was only narrowly applied as a matter of law. It did not portend impending emancipation across the empire, nor did its reach extend to either the American colonies or their West Indian neighbors where a much larger plantation economy still thrived.

It is also entirely unrealistic to speculate that Britain would have imposed emancipation in the American colonies had the war for independence gone the other way. We know this because Britain's own pathway to abolition in its remaining colonies entailed a half-century battle against intense parliamentary resistance after *Somerset*.

Simply securing a prohibition on the slave trade became a lifetime project of the abolitionist William Wilberforce, who proposed the notion in 1787, and of liberal Whig leader Charles James Fox, who brought it to a vote in 1791, only to see it go down in flames as merchant interests and West Indian planters organized to preserve the slave trade. Any student of the American Revolution will recognize the member of Parliament from Liverpool who successfully led the slave traders in opposition, for it was Banastre Tarleton, famed cavalry officer under General Cornwallis on the British side of the war.[4]

Tarleton's father and grandfather owned merchant firms in Liverpool, and directly profiteered from the slave trade. When Fox and Wilberforce's slave trade ban came to a vote he led the opposition in debate. The measure failed with 163 against and only 88 in favor.

After more than a decade of failed attempts Fox eventually persevered, steering a bill that allowed the slave trade ban through the House of Commons as one of his final acts before he died in 1806. It would take another generation for Wilberforce and Thomas Clarkson, invested in a decades-long public campaign that highlighted the horrors of the institution and assisted by a large slave uprising in Jamaica, before a full Slavery Abolition Act would clear Parliament in 1833.

Nor was Tarleton the only loyalist from the revolutionary war with a stake in slavery as an institution. Lord Dunmore, whose 1775 proclamation forms the basis of the 1619 Project's argument, comes across as a desperate political opportunist rather than a principled actor once he is examined in light of his later career. From 1787 to 1796 he served as colonial governor of the Bahamas, where he embarked on a massive and controversial building project to fortify the city of Nassau against irrational fears of foreign invasion. Dunmore used more than 600 enslaved laborers to construct a network of fortifications, including a famous 66-step staircase that they hand carved from solid rock under the threat of whipping and torture.[5] Responding to a parliamentary inquiry on the condition of the colony's slaves in 1789, Dunmore absurdly depicted them as well cared for and content with their condition.[6]

Curiously enough, a British victory in the American Revolution would have almost certainly delayed the politics of this process even further. With the American colonies still intact, planters from Virginia, the Carolinas, and Georgia would have likely joined their West Indian counterparts to obstruct any measure that weakened slavery from advancing through Parliament. Subject to greater oversight from London, the northern colonies would have had fewer direct options to eliminate the institution on their own.

These state-initiated measures came about through both legislative action and legal proceeding, including a handful of "freedom cases" that successfully deployed reasoning similar to *Somerset* to strike against the presence of slavery in New England. The most notable example occurred in Massachusetts, where an escaped slave named Quock Walker successfully used the state's new post-independence Constitution of 1780 to challenge the legality of enforcing slavery within its borders.[7]

Although they had significantly smaller slave populations than the southern states, several other northern states used the occasion of independence to move against the institution. The newly constituted state governments of Pennsylvania (1780), New Hampshire (1783), Connecticut (1784), Rhode Island (1784), and New York (1799) adopted measures for gradual but certain emancipation, usually phased in over a specified period of time or taking effect as underage enslaved persons reached legal majority. Vermont abolished slavery under its constitution as an independent republic aligned with the revolutionaries in 1777, and officially joined the United States as a free state in 1791. Antislavery delegates to the Confederation Congress were similarly able to secure a prohibition against the institution's extension under the Northwest Ordinance of 1787, ensuring that the modern-day states of Ohio, Michigan, Illinois, Wisconsin, and Indiana entered the Union as free states.[8]

While these examples do not negate the pernicious effects of slavery upon the political trajectory of the former southern colonies, they do reveal clear instances where the cause of emancipation was aided—rather than impeded—by the American Revolution. Britain's own plodding course to emancipation similarly negates an underlying premise of Hannah-Jones's depiction of the Crown as an existential threat to American slavery itself in 1776. Indeed, the reluctance of the slaveholding West Indian colonies to join those on the continent in rebellion despite repeated overtures from the Americans reveals the opposite. The planters of Jamaica, Barbados, and other Caribbean islands considered their institutions secure under the Crown—and they would remain so for another half-century.

The Verdict: The historians have a clear upper hand in disputing the portrayal of the American Revolution as an attempt to protect slavery from British-instigated abolitionism. Britain itself remained several decades away from abolition at the time of the revolution. Hannah-Jones's argument nonetheless contains kernels of truth that complicate the historians' assessment, without overturning it. Included among these are instances where Britain was involved in the emancipation of slaves during the course of the war. These events must also be balanced against the fact that American independence created new opportunities for the northern states to abolish slavery within their borders. In the end, slavery's relationship with the American Revolution was fraught with complexities that cut across the political dimensions of both sides.

2. Was Abraham Lincoln a racial colonizationist or exaggerated egalitarian?

In her lead essay, Nikole Hannah-Jones pointed to several complexities in the political beliefs of Abraham Lincoln to argue that his reputation as a racial egalitarian has been exaggerated. She points specifically to Lincoln's long-standing support for the colonization of freed slaves abroad as a corollary feature of ending slavery, including a notorious August 1862 meeting at the White House in which the president pressed this scheme upon a delegation of free African-Americans.

Elsewhere she points to grating remarks by Lincoln that questioned the possibility of attaining racial equality in the United States, and to his tepid reactions to the proposition of black citizenship at the end of the Civil War. Hannah-Jones's final assessment is not unduly harsh, but it does dampen some of the "Great Emancipator" mythology of popular perception while also questioning the extent to which Lincoln can be viewed as a philosophical egalitarian, as distinct from an anti-slavery man.

The historians' letter contests this depiction, responding that Lincoln evolved in an egalitarian direction and pointing to his embrace of an anti-slavery constitutionalism that was also shared by Frederick Douglass. Hannah-Jones, they contend, has essentially cherry-picked quotations and other examples of Lincoln's shortcomings on racial matters and presented them out of context from his life and broader philosophical principles.

Although the historians' letter to the *Times* only briefly discusses the particular details of Hannah-Jones's essay, several of the signers have individually elaborated on these claims. McPherson, Oakes, and Wilentz have all advanced various interpretations that imbue Lincoln with more radical sentiments—including on racial equality—than his words and actions evince at the surface.[9]

These arguments usually depict an element of political shrewdness at play in which Lincoln is forced to obscure his true intentions from a racist electorate until emancipation was secured or the Civil War was won. When Hannah-Jones points to policies such as colonization, or to problematic speeches by Lincoln that suggest a less-than-egalitarian view of African-Americans, the historians respond that these charges miss a deeper political context. And in their telling, that context largely serves an exonerative purpose.

The historians' treatment of colonization is probably the foremost example of how they deploy this argument around Lincoln. McPherson was one of the main originators of what has become known as the "lullaby thesis."[10] According to this thesis, Lincoln only advanced racially charged policies such as colonization to lull a reluctant populace into accepting the "strong pill" of emancipation. Once emancipation was achieved, McPherson and the other lullaby theorists maintain, Lincoln promptly retreated from these racially fraught auxiliary positions—a claim supposedly evidenced by Lincoln's omission of colonizationist language from the final version of the Emancipation Proclamation of January 1, 1863. Colonization is therefore reduced to a political stratagem, insincerely advanced to clear the way for emancipation.

Wilentz echoes McPherson on this claim, and at times presses it even further. In 2009 he published a vicious and dismissive attack on Henry Louis Gates, Jr., after the eminent African-American scholar called upon historians to update their consideration of Lincoln's colonization policies and consider the possibility that they sincerely reflected his beliefs.[11]

Gates's interpretation was far from radical or disparaging of Lincoln.[12] He correctly noted that the evidentiary record on Lincoln's colonization programs had substantially expanded since the time that McPherson and others posited the lullaby thesis in the second half of the 20th century. Wilentz's counter-argument offered little to counter the new evidence, relying instead on invocations of authority from leading scholars including himself.[13]

When viewed in light of these and other recent archival discoveries, the lullaby thesis and similar variants as espoused by the signers of the letter may be conclusively rejected.

Lincoln's sincere belief in colonization may be documented from the earliest days of his political career as a Henry Clay Whig in Illinois to a succession of failed attempts to launch colonization projects during his presidency.[14] Furthermore, the claim that Lincoln abandoned colonization after the Emancipation Proclamation in January 1863 is directly belied by another year of sustained diplomatic negotiations with the governments of Great Britain and the Netherlands as Lincoln sought to secure suitable locales in their Caribbean colonies.[15]

Lincoln's proactive support for colonization kept it alive until at least 1864 when a series of political setbacks induced Congress to strip away the program's funding against the president's wishes. A fair amount of evidence suggests Lincoln intended to revive the project in his second term, and new discoveries pertaining to long-missing colonization records from Lincoln's presidency continue to be made.[16]

I won't belabor the point further, save to note that the evidence of Lincoln's sincere support for colonization is overwhelming.[17]

This finding carries with it the substantial caveat that Lincoln did not pursue this course out of personal racial animosity. Quite the contrary, his public and private statements consistently link the policy to his personal fears that former slave owners would continue to oppress African-Americans after the Civil War. The colonization component of his solution was a racially retrograde and paternalistic reflection of its time, but it also revealed Lincoln's awareness of the challenges that lay ahead in his second term. Given that Lincoln's presidency and life were cut short, we will never know what that term would have brought. And while there are subtle clues of Lincoln's migration toward greater racial inclusivity in other areas—for example, the extension of suffrage to black soldiers—the record on colonization is in clear tension with the arguments advanced by the 1619 Project's critics.

The Verdict: Nikole Hannah-Jones has the clear upper hand here. Her call to evaluate Lincoln's record through problematic racial policies such as colonization reflects greater historical nuance and closer attention to the evidentiary record, including new developments in Lincoln scholarship. The

Fact-Checking the 1619 Project and Its Critics | 31

historians' counter-arguments reflect a combination of outdated evidence and the construction of apocryphal exonerative narratives such as the lullaby thesis around colonization.

3. Did slavery drive America's economic growth and the emergence of American capitalism?

Matthew Desmond's 1619 Project contribution has been at the center of the firestorm since the day it was published.[18] The main thrust of this article holds that slavery was the primary driver of American economic growth in the 19th century, and that it infused its brutality into American capitalism today. The resulting thesis is overtly ideological and overtly anti-capitalist, seeking to enlist slavery as an explanatory mechanism for a long list of grievances he has against the Republican Party's positions on health care, taxation, and labor regulation in the present day.

The five historians directly challenged the historical accuracy of Desmond's thesis. By presenting "supposed direct connections between slavery and modern corporate practices," they note, the 1619 Project's editors "have so far failed to establish any empirical veracity or reliability" of these claims "and have been seriously challenged by other historians." The historians' letter further chastises the *Times* for extending its "imprimatur and credibility" to these claims.

Each of these criticisms rings true.

Desmond's thesis relies exclusively on scholarship from a hotly contested school of thought known as the New History of Capitalism (NHC). Although NHC scholars often present their work as cutting-edge explorations into the relationship between capitalism and slavery, they have not fared well under scrutiny from outside their own ranks.[19]

Other scholars, including several leading economic historians, have reached similar conclusions, finding very little merit in this body of work. As discussed in previous sections of this book, the NHC camp frequently struggles with basic economic concepts and statistics, has a clear track record of misrepresenting historical evidence to bolster its arguments, and has adopted a bizarre and insular practice of refusing to answer substantive scholarly criticisms from non-NHC scholars—including from opposite ends of the political spectrum.[20]

32 | *The 1619 Project Myth*

While most criticisms of Desmond's thesis focus upon these broader problems in the NHC literature, the *Times* has done practically nothing to address the issues involved. Hannah-Jones herself admitted to being unaware of the controversy surrounding the NHC material until I pointed it out to her shortly after the 1619 Project appeared in print.[21] From that time until the present the 1619 Project has almost intentionally disengaged from the problems with Desmond's essay—and so it remains in Silverstein's response.

Although the *Times* editor attempted to answer most of the other specific criticisms from the historians, he was conspicuously silent on the subject of Desmond's thesis. Hannah-Jones has similarly shown little interest in revisiting this piece or responding to specific criticisms of the NHC literature. Meanwhile, the *Times* continues to extend this defective body of academic work its imprimatur and credibility, exactly as the historians' letter charges.

The Verdict: This one goes conclusively to the five historians. Echoing other critics, the historians point to serious and substantive defects with Matthew Desmond's thesis about the economics of slavery, and with the project's overreliance on the contested New History of Capitalism literature. By contrast, the *Times* has completely failed to offer a convincing response to this criticism—or really any response at all.

4. Did the 1619 Project seek adequate scholarly guidance in preparing its work?

Moving beyond the content of the project itself, the historians' letter raises a broader criticism of the scholarly vetting behind the 1619 Project. They charge that the *Times* used an "opaque" fact-checking process, marred by "selective transparency" about the names and qualifications of scholars involved. They further suggest that Hannah-Jones and other *Times* editors did not solicit sufficient input from experts on the subjects they covered—a point that several of the signers reiterated in their individual interviews.

Silverstein takes issue with this criticism, noting that they "consulted with numerous scholars of African-American history and related fields" and subjected the resulting articles to rigorous fact-checking. He also specifically identifies five scholars involved in these consultations who each contributed a piece to the 1619 Project. They are Mehrsa Baradaran, Matthew Desmond, Kevin Kruse, Tiya Miles, and Khalil G. Muhammed.

Each of these scholars brings relevant areas of expertise to aspects of the larger project. The listed names, however, are noticeably light when it comes to historians of the subject areas that the critics describe as deficient, namely the period from the American Revolution to the Civil War or roughly 1775 to 1865.

Of the five named academic consultants, only Miles possesses a clear scholarly expertise in this period of history. Her contributions to the project —three short vignettes about slavery, business, and migration—are not disputed by the five historian critics, and do not appear to have elicited any significant criticism.[22] Rather, they have been well-received as abbreviated distillations of her scholarly work for a popular audience.

The true oddity of the group remains Matthew Desmond, a sociologist who specializes in present day race-relations. Although Desmond was given the task of writing the 1619 Project's main article on the economics of slavery, he does not appear to have any scholarly expertise in either economics or the history of slavery. None of his scholarly publications are on subjects related to the period between 1775 and 1865.[23] Indeed most of his work focuses on the 20th century or later. As a result, Desmond approaches his 1619 Project essay entirely as a second-hand disseminator of the aforementioned claims from the problematic New History of Capitalism literature.

The other three named consultants—Kruse, Baradaran, and Muhammad —all specialize in more recent areas of history or social science, so none of them could plausibly claim an expertise in the period that the five historians focus their criticisms upon.

Barring the revelation of additional names, it appears that the 1619 Project neglected to adequately vet its material covering slavery during the period between the American Revolution and the Civil War. Its editors also appear to have assigned the primary article on this period to a writer who may possess expertise in other areas of social science involving race, but who is not qualified for the specific task of assessing slavery's economic dimensions.

Although Silverstein attempted to defuse this angle of the historians' criticism, he ended up only affirming its validity. Since the period in question encompasses several of the most important events in the history of slavery, this oversight harms the project's credibility in the areas where the five historians are highly regarded experts.

The Verdict: The historians have a valid complaint about deficiencies of scholarly guidance for the 1619 Project's treatment of the period between the American Revolution and the Civil War. This comparative lack of scholarly input for the years between 1775 and 1865 stands in contrast with the *Times*'s heavy use of scholars who specialize in more recent dimensions of race in the United States. It is worth noting that the 1619 Project has received far less pushback on its materials about the 20th century and present day—areas that are more clearly within the scholarly competencies of the named consultants.

6

The Case for Retracting Matthew Desmond's 1619 Project Essay

In a series of exchanges with 1619 Project editor Nikole Hannah-Jones, I first raised the possibility of the Times *issuing a correction to the many factual errors in Matthew Desmond's essay on capitalism and slavery. As I noted at the time, substantively addressing the problems with this piece alone would resolve several of the most severe criticisms of the project as a whole. It would also be consistent with the* Times's *reputation for vigorous fact-checking.*

The faults with Desmond's essay extended beyond the interpretive disputes of the other contributions, and included both factual errors and misrepresentations of claims that appeared in scholarly works of history and economic history. After multiple attempts to pursue these corrections through the Times *yielded little response and continued dismissiveness about the problems by Hannah-Jones, I summarized the main faults in an essay calling for the retraction of Desmond's piece.*

SINCE THE OUTSET of the 1619 Project controversy detailed throughout this book, I have consistently argued that the overwhelming majority of the project's problems derive from a single featured essay: Matthew Desmond's piece on capitalism and slavery.[1]

Desmond's essay advances an explicit anti-capitalist political message that's rooted in a fundamental misreading of economic history. Although he repurposes the concept with an anti-slavery message, Desmond essentially attempts to rehabilitate "King Cotton" ideology, a long-discredited piece of pro-slavery propaganda from the Confederate era. He also ignores the aforementioned intellectual history of capitalism, including the strong historical association between laissez-faire theorists and abolitionism.

I'd like to take a look at another dimension of the problems in Desmond's essay: its errors of historical fact and its misuse of historical sources.

In doing so, it is important to recognize that there are still faults with other contributions to the 1619 Project. Its lead essay still exaggerates British anti-slavery elements during the American Revolution, repurposing independence as a pro-slavery movement.[2] But these faults are not irremediable. They could be addressed by relaxing the claim or injecting greater nuance into the discussion, should the *Times* exhibit an inclination to place historical accuracy above politics.

Desmond's argument, however, is riddled with factual error and dubious scholarly interpretations that warrant severely discounting the piece as a whole.

Let's consider those problems.

A Faulty Genealogy

Desmond begins his argument by asserting a direct lineal descent from the violent and coercive operations of the plantation system to the business practices of the modern economy. As he contends, "recently, historians have pointed persuasively to the gnatty fields of Georgia and Alabama, to the cotton houses and slave auction blocks, as the birthplace of America's low-road approach to capitalism." The historians he refers to here are almost exclusively drawn from the highly contested "New History of Capitalism" (NHC) school, and many of its leading contributors are featured in his essay.

Desmond's reliance on such a narrow historiographical echo chamber is itself problematic, given how many scholars outside of the NHC reject its claims and given the documentation of errors affecting its core claims. We may nonetheless follow his claimed genealogical progression from the plantation to the modern economy. The effect of this alleged infusion, Desmond therefore contends, is to instill modern capitalism with a foundational "brutality" that can only be rectified by adopting a litany of economic policy interventions that bear striking resemblance to the progressive wing of the Democratic Party today.

The stated genealogy is presented as a matter of fact. Desmond invokes the imagery of a modern corporation where "everything is tracked, recorded and analyzed, via vertical reporting systems, double-entry record-keeping and precise quantification," then asserts that "many of these techniques that we now take for granted were developed by and for large plantations."

"When an accountant depreciates an asset to save on taxes or when a mid-level manager spends an afternoon filling in rows and columns on an Excel spreadsheet," he continues, "they are repeating business procedures whose roots twist back to slave-labor camps." By direct implication, modern capitalism carries that same moral stain with it.

There are immediate problems with Desmond's historical narrative. The history of double-entry bookkeeping and business measurement predates plantation slavery by several centuries, with origins that are directly traceable to the banking families of late medieval Italy.[3] Desmond seems not to understand the accounting function of depreciation, which arose mainly in the railroad industry as a mechanism for distributing the distortive effects of large replacement purchases on machinery that underwent constant wear and tear.[4]

Nor are the tools of measurement and finance distinctly capitalistic, as their attempted adaptation to the centralized planning of the Soviet Union and other 20th-century communist states attests. Most attempts to operationalize socialist economic planning depend by necessity on the complex quantification of resource allocation, or attempts at input-output modeling of inter-industry relationships, usually adopted as an alternative to the obviated role of the price mechanism in decentralized allocation.[5]

But even more problematically, Desmond's claim does not match his own stated source, Caitlin Rosenthal's 2018 book *Accounting for Slavery*.[6] While Rosenthal does investigate the historical use of accounting practices on the plantation with informative insights into how slave owners made their institution profitable, she attaches a substantial caveat at the outset of her book:

> This is not an origins story. I did not find a simple path where slaveholders' paper spreadsheets evolved into Microsoft Excel.

The plain language of this caveat expressly disavows the genealogical interpretation that Desmond assigns to her work, even using the very same

38 | *The 1619 Project Myth*

example of Microsoft Excel to convey her rejection. In short, the 1619 Project inverts its source's claimed purpose.

When I recently pointed this contradiction out to the *Times*, the newspaper's editors indicated that they were standing by Desmond's claim nonetheless and suggested that doing so now meets with Rosenthal's own post hoc concurrence. Given that her publisher is also now touting Desmond's passage as an endorsement of this book, one is left to wonder why this caveat was included if it is going to be abandoned with such nonchalance.

The alteration carries substantial implications for Rosenthal's thesis. As presented in its original form, *Accounting for Slavery* documents the unsurprising but historically interesting fact that slave owners managed their plantations by adapting then-modern accounting and financial practices found elsewhere in the business community to their own horrid institution.

When repurposed as a genealogy, however, this thesis falls apart for want of evidence. Rosenthal's work does not show that the specific accounting practices of the plantations were transmitted to modern Wall Street, or that later businessmen learned their trades specifically from slavery's financial innovations, as opposed to common financial and accounting practices that long predate the American plantation system. If accepted, Desmond's rendering of *Accounting for Slavery* would damage its own scholarly contribution as a work of history by stretching its evidence far beyond what the book's contents and documentation either claim or support. Yet that's the reading the *Times* appears to be sticking with.

Even in this simple presentation, Desmond's spin on Rosenthal's work exhibits the telltale characteristics of the genetic fallacy, wherein an unsavory origin is said to be a discrediting of a position in the present. But Desmond's origin story is also wrong.

Illustrative of this fallacy, he quotes NHC historians Sven Beckert and Seth Rockman to assert that "American slavery is necessarily imprinted on the DNA of American capitalism." Beckert and Rockman's genetic claim would have come as a great surprise, if not a source of outrage, to the slaveholders of the late antebellum period. As mentioned earlier, leading pro-slavery theorist George Fitzhugh wrote in 1854 that the tenets of free market capitalism were "at war with all kinds of slavery, for they in fact assert that individuals and peoples prosper most when governed least."[7] The depiction of slavery as capitalistic also chafes with the most developed ideological justifications that Southern radicals made for their economic system—a system built upon a coerced hierarchy of laborers forced to do menial tasks under the paternalistic direction of quasi-feudal plantation owners.[8]

This leaves Desmond's historical account fraught through with factual and interpretive errors. His attempt to tie slavery to modern accounting misses the latter's known and separate origins, misrepresents accounting and measurement as uniquely capitalistic, and directly inverts the disavowal of an origin story in its own cited source.[9] It's safe to say that his thesis is off to a poor start.

A Misrepresented Statistical Claim

Taking his own false genealogy of modern accounting as a given, Desmond next turns to its claimed economic implications for the plantation system. To illustrate the effect, he points to a stunning statistic:

> During the 60 years leading up to the Civil War, the daily amount of cotton picked per enslaved worker increased 2.3 percent a year. That means that in 1862, the average enslaved fieldworker picked not 25 percent or 50 percent as much but 400 percent as much cotton than his or her counterpart did in 1801.

The implication is clear. Desmond seeks to convey that "capitalist" business practices allowed plantation masters to forcibly extract the maximum amount of productivity from their enslaved workforce to such a degree that it causally drove the rapid expansion of the American cotton industry in the early 19th century. Cotton output, he contends, arose directly from a symbiotic convergence of capitalism and the whip.

The underlying statistic is nominally accurate insofar as American cotton production grew almost fourfold between 1800 and the Civil War. But Desmond has also repeated a severe misrepresentation of this statistic's source.

The 400 percent increase estimate comes from a 2008 article by economists Alan Olmstead and Paul Rhode, and reflects their calculation of yearly cotton picking rates from almost 150 sets of plantation records.[10] Yet Olmstead and Rhode do not attribute this production increase to a devil's bargain between double-entry bookkeeping and systematized beatings of the slaves.

40 | *The 1619 Project Myth*

Instead, they present clear evidence of a very different explanation. American planters improved their crop through biological innovation, such as creating hybrid seed strains that yielded more cotton, were easier to pick, and were more resistant to disease. As Olmstead and Rhode conclude:

> Technological changes revolutionized southern cotton production in the 60 years preceding the Civil War. The amount of cotton a typical slave picked per day increased about 2.3 percent per year due, primarily, to the introduction and perfection of superior cotton varieties.

Although the two economists support this technological explanation with extensive statistical evidence, Desmond and the NHC scholars he relies on ignore it and append their own alternative spin to Olmstead and Rhode's data. Instead of seed improvements, they contend that the 400 percent increase arose from a systematized and quantified process of whipping meant to extract greater labor from the slaves.

Desmond gets this alternative interpretation directly from NHC historian Ed Baptist. According to Baptist, the Olmstead and Rhode statistics attest to "an economy whose bottom gear was torture." By tracking individual slave production, he contends, slave drivers were essentially able to calibrate their torture to maximize and increase cotton picking rates over time. As Desmond describes it, "The violence [of slavery] was neither arbitrary nor gratuitous. It was rational, capitalistic, all part of the plantation's design."

The "calibrated torture" thesis is a central claim of Baptist's 2015 book *The Half Has Never Been Told,* itself one of the foundational texts of the NHC genre.[11] Turning to Baptist's book, we find clearly that he too enlisted Olmstead and Rhode's 2008 paper for his evidence of the fourfold increase in cotton output before the Civil War, even reprinting one of their main graphs on page 127 of his book and another of their tables on page 129.

Baptist's book is an unscholarly mess of misinterpreted data, misrepresented sources, and empirical incompetence. In proclaiming the novelty of its own "never told" story, he also constructs a bizarre strawman of the scholarly literature on the economics of slavery before his own work. As Baptist writes on page 129 of his book, the claim that slavery was less efficient than free labor is "a point of dogma that most historians and economists have accepted."

The Case for Retracting Matthew Desmond's 1619 Project Essay | 41

In reality, most economic historians have associated economic efficiency as well as profitability with slavery since a landmark article by Alfred Conrad and John R. Meyer argued this position in 1958.[12] The relationship between slavery, efficiency, and profitability is the subject of a vast subsequent literature that Baptist almost entirely ignores.[13] As we can already see, his book is essentially arguing against a phantasm of his own imagination.

The problems similarly extend to Baptist's treatment of the Olmstead and Rhode data. Although Baptist uses the economists' statistics, he conveniently omits their evidence that cotton production growth arose from biological innovation in seed strains. Instead he supplants it with his own explanation, the "calibrated torture" thesis that Desmond then repeats. In the NHC telling, the 400 percent growth in cotton output arose from "ratcheting" production rates upward through tracked and mathematized beatings of the slaves who picked the crop.

Baptist's sleight of hand was not lost upon the economists. In 2018 Olmstead and Rhode published a withering rebuttal of Baptist's book, using additional records from plantations to empirically debunk his "calibrated torture" argument.[14] Rather than corresponding to mathematized whipping—a claim that Baptist also makes by altering and distorting the text of historical slave narratives to make them fit his thesis—actual cotton picking rates from the Olmstead and Rhode data clearly follow a seasonal pattern corresponding to the annual crop cycle. As the economists write:

> Recall that Baptist has embraced our data showing a roughly four fold increase in average cotton picking rates over the antebellum years. These data only reported plantation yearly averages. If we turn up the power of our microscope and look at the daily data for individual slaves that we used to construct the plantation averages, a whole new world appears that allows us to investigate empirically the effect of current picking on future picking. There is no evidence of ratcheting. Over the course of a year picking rates formed an inverted "U" going up to a peak period and then falling significantly.

In short, Baptist's thesis not only misrepresents the evidence from Olmstead and Rhode, his own cited data source—it also misunderstands the numbers behind that source.

Baptist, much to the discredit of his professionalism, has subsequently adopted a strategy of refusing to engage with Olmstead and Rhode's rebuttal. Instead he brushes it aside and persists as if his own thesis is uninterrupted and unaltered in the face of clear contradictory evidence.

Although the 1619 Project's editors have been circumspect about revealing the scholars they consulted on the project, it is becoming increasingly clear that Baptist heavily influenced and likely advised Desmond's essay. Desmond essentially adopts *The Half Has Never Been Told* as the basis of his economic interpretation, and of the aforementioned statistics. It therefore casually repeats Baptist's errors and misrepresentations of Olmstead and Rhode's work.

Olmstead and Rhode's critique of Baptist falls squarely among the highest-profile academic debates of the last decade. In 2016 it broke away from the confines of academic journals and into mainstream journalism, with even the *Washington Post* running an essay on the dispute.[15]

Curiously, the 1619 Project's editors appear to have completely missed this dispute. When I asked her about Desmond's over-reliance on Ed Baptist's debunked claims, project editor Nikole Hannah-Jones responded, "Economists dispute a few of Baptist's calculations but not the book itself nor its thesis."[16]

Olmstead offers a very different assessment: "Edward Baptist's study of capitalism and slavery is flawed beyond repair."[17] And as we've now seen, Desmond's 1619 Project essay lifted its main empirical argument from Baptist and grafted it onto a false genealogy that purports to derive modern accounting practices from lineal "roots" in the plantation system.

It would seem, too, that Desmond's essay is flawed beyond repair.

As the *New York Times* often presents itself as a stickler for corrections in the name of ensuring factual and interpretive accuracy, substantial portions of Desmond's essay warrant retraction—including its main thesis linking modern capitalism to slavery.

7

A Comment on the "New" History of American Capitalism

This longer paper, adapted from my published work on the subject, contains a historiographic discussion of the New History of Capitalism (NHC) literature. This emergent genre of historical scholarship forms the basis of Matthew Desmond's essay and argument. In my paper, I discuss the problems of the NHC literature, including its use of defective definitions for the term "capitalism" and its embrace of a heavily anti-capitalistic ideological lens.

OVER HALF A century has passed since F. A. Hayek called attention to an "emotional aversion to 'capitalism'" within the history profession. He traced this criticism to a persistent belief that the industrial-competitive mechanisms of the modern era reached a sustained and unprecedented state of economic expansion at the expense of society's weakest members. If the economic enrichment since the industrial revolution was achieved on the backs of the poor, the economically ravaged, and the exploited, it is but a short step to brush aside the empirically attested abundance of "capitalism" as a tainted good. Both then and now, such zero sum thinking depends upon an almost intentional myopia that constructs its evidence selectively to fit its already-accepted diagnosis of capitalism's ills. Yet its persistence constitutes the "one supreme myth which more than any other has served to discredit the economic system to which we owe our present-day civilization."[1] Perceptions

---

An earlier version of this chapter appeared in Michael Douma and Phillip W. Magness, eds. 2017. *What Is Classical Liberal History?* Lexington Books.

of the past—including mistaken ones—are a heavy epistemic weight upon policy decisions in the present.

Simultaneously alarming and prescient, Hayek's description still rings true on many counts. Inequality in particular retains a persistent place in historical treatments of economic events, including a tendency to view the allocation of society's wealth as an end unto itself, or as a destabilizing causal mechanism behind a multitude of other social ills, as opposed to a measurement of other factors of growth and fiscal policy. While the topic is itself unobjectionable and even a necessary tool for assessing the distributional effects of economic outcomes, the historical study of inequality is almost always paired with prescriptive political arguments for redistributive policy making or vindications of past examples of the same.[2]

The history profession's attention shifted away from economic history in the second half of the 20th century, ceding this turf to an increasingly quantitative economic history subfield housed in economics departments. Mainstream historical interest in economic matters resurged with a vengeance following the financial crisis of 2008. The product is a loosely defined assemblage of economically themed research, sometimes referred to as the "New History of Capitalism" (NHC).[3] Although branded with the moniker "new," a number of its defining elements are not all that novel. While it would be a mistake to attribute ideological uniformity to this growing subfield, the core characteristics of Hayek's half-century-old diagnosis are abundant in this recent body of literature. Several leading works of NHC scholarship approach "capitalism" as a cohesive societal order or system, and an eminently blameworthy one at that. Themes of physical expropriation, distributional inequality, labor mistreatment, and economic exploitation linger in the background of much of this work, and—perhaps above all other concerns—attempts to causally link slavery to the emergence of a capitalist economic "system" are particularly strong.

In doing so, the distinctive feature of the NHC genre is not actually its claimed revival of a neglected set of topics that never really left the discussion. Historians have long studied questions of economic inequality and distribution, and the socio-economic dimensions of slavery have been a pre-eminent focus of historical attention for decades. Rather, what distinguishes recent works under the NHC moniker is their aggressive embrace of what Hayek diagnosed over half a century ago as a latent bias of academic historians. In attempting to study "capitalism," these works often begin from aggressively anti-capitalistic priors and peddle in the practice of infusing their authors' own ideological distastes for "capitalism," often broadly construed yet poorly defined, to long-familiar topics of historical study.

The tensions between NHC and classical liberalism are numerous and warrant consideration in detail, though one general development since Hayek's time suggests that capitalism's defenders enjoy an improved scholarly position in the present day even as the growth of the NHC movement portends invigorated hostilities. The intervening decades have yielded a vibrant scholarly literature on what Deirdre McCloskey has termed the "Great Enrichment"—the historically unparalleled expansion in the wealth and well-being of ordinary human lives that has occurred since roughly 1800. The attributed causes of this process are multifaceted and sometimes in tension with each other, though its major characteristics are situated somewhere between an emerging ethical and cultural valuation of economic production in the late 18th century, the existence of favorable legal and institutional characteristics, the improved access to and dissemination of requisite knowledge for productive processes, and the broader influence of the enlightenment upon the intellectual environment of the early industrial revolution.[4] Each offers a plausible interpretation of what might be called a capitalist age, for lack of a better term, rejecting the zero-sum disposition of recent NHC contributions and calling our attention to its empirically undeniable abundance.

A distinctive characteristic of the history of the "Great Enrichment" is its natural interaction with a number of classical liberal insights, particularly from economics. Its story rests upon an empirical observation of rapidly improved human well-being and attempts to discern its causal mechanisms not from any narrative plan or singular ideology, but through spontaneously organized exchange in a favorable cultural and institutional environment. Its story is not premised upon an idealized conception of "capitalism" or the denial of historical experiences in its wake, injustices among them, but rather the humility to ask whether such a diverse array of events can be legitimately ascribed to a single system.

Capitalism was not proclaimed, adopted, imposed, or arrived at as a moment in time. In the classical liberal sense, capitalism simply refers to a set of conditions and circumstances that are favorable to voluntary human interactions and that are distinguished by their absence of a centralized design. It describes a number of attributes in an economy—a freedom in the exchange and movement of goods and people, a general recognition of the validity of private property and a stable and discernable system of contracts built upon it, a cultural environment of toleration for choice and celebration of discovery, and a worldview that—at least in its professed values—deprecates forceful predation, whether by other economic actors or the power of the nation-state. A classical liberal history of capitalism is therefore a history of the conditions that permit free exchange and discovery, and with them the witnessed results of the past two hundred years.

The divergence between this conceptualization and the emerging NHC literature is profound. It presents two distinctive stories: a classical liberal capitalism as a descriptive term for spontaneously ordering interactions of the past, and an ideological capitalism that quite literally serves as a lightning rod for faults and blame in interpreting the past's many ills. What follows in this discussion is a brief examination of some of the main features and themes of the NHC literature and its tensions with the former classical liberal conceptualization. What this framing portends for the historical discussion of capitalism remains to be seen, and will likely attract much scholarly attention in the coming years. As this discussion will highlight, many of the differences between the two approaches stem from a disciplinary divide between historians and economists. One consequence of this divide may be seen in a number of profound methodological and definitional imprecisions afflicting the recent NHC genre, setting up the conditions in which strong ideological priors have become a primary motive for this line of research.

Between Divergent Paths

The study of history in the latter part of the 20th century was distinguished by a methodological divide between an older approach rooted in evidentiary empiricism and an emergent attention to social history, and particularly that of group identities based on racial, class, and gender lines. Few subfields were more directly affected by this divide than economic history. Once an inter-disciplinary domain that attracted collaborative conversations between economists and historians, the subfield was largely swept up in the "cliometric revolution" that took hold in the early 1960s. In some sense an extreme form of quantitative empiricism in its own right, the cliometric approach saw the emerging tools of statistics, econometrics, and economic modeling applied to historical analysis. Social history in turn pulled the attention of many traditional historians away from an ever-specialized discussion of economic matters, albeit with occasional forays on a topic by topic basis. Slavery was one such example where the methodological pathways between economics and historians diverged sharply.[5]

Some of the earliest cliometric work applied heavy data analysis to the ever-topical economic question of slavery's economics, and particularly its profitability. The economic theories of a century prior had conventionally asserted an intuitive tension between slavery and capitalism premised on free labor. In addition to its moral dimensions, slavery removed the economic incentive of the slave to better his product and introduced a number of inefficiencies to its productive processes—particularly those measured in lost opportunity.[6] The empirical investigation of slavery's profitability in the second half of the 20th century shifted this discussion. While the new empirical literature did not establish slavery's immunity from the economic inefficiencies with which it had been charged, and sometimes punted on this question entirely, it did show the economic viability of plantation production in the late antebellum. The economists, it seems, had uncovered a reason in profitability that explained slavery's persistence. The evidence, at least on that point, ran counter to a somewhat wishful 19th-century belief among some abolition-minded economists that the plantation system, if left to its own devices, would be outcompeted and die a natural death.

In a sense, the study of the economic dimensions of slavery is a microcosm for the subsequent compartmentalization of economic history onto divergent trajectories.[7] The cliometric end of this genre peaked with Robert Fogel and Stanley Engerman's landmark *Time on the Cross* in 1973, notable for the out-pouring of respondents it provoked among historians and economists alike as well as its controversial but data-driven substantiation of the plantation system's profitability. This last point instigated something of a sea change in economic history, as it ran counter to both elements of an existing historical literature on slavery and the aforementioned conventional assumptions of economic thought about slave labor in the 19th century. Curiously, the ensuing debate over slavery's profitability—and with it an oft-implied but sometimes contested claim of slavery's economic efficiency—was never quite settled, though conflicting claims of victory persist among the cliometric economists and traditional historians alike.[8]

It is likely no coincidence that the slave economy is a central focus of NHC scholarship.[9] The causal relationships implied by much of this literature are remarkably fluid, such that capitalism is simultaneously an enabling prerequisite of large-scale (and race-based) plantation slavery, as distinct from the ancient world institution, as well as its most visible beneficiary—an economic system propelled to modernity upon the backs of the slaves. In either case, many NHC scholars advance a politically tinged subtext that effectively saddles capitalism with both cause and credit for slavery's economic output and therefore, by implication, its moral price tag.

The themes of these contributions differ somewhat, with emphases that range from tracing the global reach and economic uses of plantation-derived products to the specific labor practices that were deployed to extract production from enslaved persons. The method of analysis is largely rooted in social observation and an archive-sustained story. Market-wide data interpretation takes a back seat to multi-method narrative. At its best, historical work of this type teases observations about slavery's production from the stories of individual plantations and shippers, the testimonies of former slaves where they exist, and the descriptive indicators of life on the plantation. The economic reach of slavery's output and other plantation-linked activities in shipping, finance, and production thus become the evidence of slavery's own centrality to the economic system in which it operated.

Despite methodological differences in assembling its evidence and interpreting its findings, a recurring feature of the NHC literature is that it arrives at one strikingly similar position as the economists. Both largely agree on slavery's profitability.[10] And both advance a rejection of at least the simplified forms of the older classical economic—and, to some degree, classical liberal—conclusion that slavery was unsuited for industrial capitalism on account of its comparative inefficiency to free labor.

It is all the more curious that several primary works of the NHC literature in the last five years appear to be only nominally aware of, or at least inatten-

A Comment on the "New" History of American Capitalism | 49

tive to, the discussions surrounding older cliometric and derivative economic investigations of the same topic, even where they drifted into the debates of the mainstream history profession in the 1970s and 80s.

To the contrary, much of the NHC work on slavery seems to be enamored with its own claims of novelty—of telling a "never told" story that has in fact appeared many times before, and that even bears a striking resemblance to the old "King Cotton" arguments that were advanced by pro-slavery radicals and Confederate nationalists in the 19th century. Consider the following excerpt from an 1856 tract:[11]

> Slavery is not an isolated system, but is so mingled with the business of the world, that it derives facilities from the most innocent transactions. Capital and labor, in Europe and America, are largely employed in the manufacture of cotton. These goods, to a great extent, may be seen freighting every vessel, from Christian nations, that traverses the seas of the globe; and filling the warehouses and shelves of the merchants over two-thirds of the world. By the industry, skill, and enterprise employed in the manufacture of cotton, mankind are better clothed; their comfort better promoted; general industry more highly stimulated; commerce more widely extended; and civilization more rapidly advanced than in any preceding age.

But for slight idiosyncrasies of tone and terminology, this cotton-centric accounting of global political economy at the middle of the 19th century could be mistaken for the primary arguments of NHC historians Sven Beckert and Edward Baptist. Beckert, for example, places a cotton-centric "war capitalism" that extends its reach into "insurance, finance, and shipping" as well as "public institutions such as government credit, money itself, and national defense." Baptist depicts a cotton-driven economic empire where slavery's reach drives everything from shipping, to "insurance and interest paid on commercial credit," to the "purchase of land, the cost of credit for such purchases, the pork and the corn bought at the river landings," to "money spent by mill-workers and Illinois hog farmers, the wages paid to steamboat workers, and the revenues yielded by investments made with the profits of the merchants, manufacturers, and slave traders who derived some or all of their income either directly or indirectly from the southwestern fields," to the clothing and toolmakers who supplied the plantations, to, of course, the vast sums of money invested in the slaves themselves.[12]

NHC scholars have not simply stumbled into a long-running debate about the efficiency of slave labor. They have also somewhat accidentally adopted an economic interpretation that finds its primary historical champions in the late antebellum bluster of James Henry Hammond, and the failed economic strategy of the Confederacy's diplomatic overtures to Europe.[13]

The ensuing NHC–cliometric divide has become pronounced and, at times, embittered.[14] Based on the sheer weight of evidence, the data-driven economic historians have often gained the upper hand by highlighting basic errors of empirical interpretation. Economists Alan Olmstead and Paul Rhode severely chastised the NHC literature for misusing historical cotton production data, including statistics that were derived from their own work. In another revealing indicator of the divide, economist Bradley Hansen noted a basic conceptual misunderstanding in NHC scholar Edward Baptist's attempt to calculate the percentage of the antebellum United States' gross domestic product that derived from slavery. Unaware of basic national income accounting practices in differentiating input costs from final goods, Baptist inadvertently double- and perhaps triple-counted cotton-derived products until he reached an empirically unsupported figure that attributed nearly half of the United States' economic output in 1836 to plantation slavery.[15]

While episodes of this sort point to a specific shortcoming in the NHC literature, itself enabled by a predisposition toward "evidence" that appears to confirm a central link between slavery and capitalism, they also show the failure of even basic economic insights to penetrate the process of peer reviewing mainstream historical works that make economic claims. While it might be tempting to fault the confirmation biases of the historians' engagement with data, and the ideological undertones of their work suggests as much, another part of the problem derives from the methodological rift with the economists.

Cliometric research comes with a steep learning curve that can, at times, render its findings inaccessible to scholars who lack intensive training in advanced econometric techniques and statistical analysis. This obstacle extends well beyond the economics of slavery, leading to cases where parallel but divergent literatures emerge on either methodological divide of the same historical subject, largely in isolation from each other. For a simple illustration, consider the widespread enthusiasm that most historians show for Franklin Roosevelt's New Deal as an effective and necessary response to the Great Depression. Almost unbeknownst to them, a parallel literature in economic history largely holds that many of these same policies as well as other lesser known "relief" measures inadvertently impeded recovery and likely prolonged the Great Depression.[16]

The divide often produces competing claimants to accuracy, even where less dissimilar positions result. Economists embrace data as a benchmark of social-scientific methods to test and validate specific claims about the past. The traditional historians in turn retort, with some validity, that the data-heavy modeling on the other side of the divide has its own limitations. For one, it can artificially constrain historical inquiry to topics where identifiable quantitative metrics exist. There are no serialized archives of the trade volume of the Ostrogothic Kingdom after all, though much else might be said about the economies of late antiquity and early medieval Europe from surviving manuscript sources and even archaeological evidence. Second, the overly cliometric emphasis of some economic history outlets often comes at the expense of the deep contextual detail that narrative historians utilize to interpret events—a point that Baptist has enlisted to his defense in the slavery debate.

These concerns are neither recent nor unfamiliar to the number crunchers of the economics profession's historical subfields. Some two decades ago, economic historian Avner Greif cautioned that the dominant framework of the neoclassical model is self-limiting in its extension to historical events. In searching for markets to analyze, it imposes ahistorical theoretical assumptions about individual preferences, technology, factor endowments, and market institutions to historical events. Greif noted the effects of this emphasis upon economic history in the period since the cliometric revolution. It appeared in the neglect of "issues that were traditionally the focus of economic historians" before the emergence of quantitative dominance. Lost were historical inquiries into "the nature and role of non-market institutions, culture, entrepreneurship, technological and organizational innovation, politics, social factors, distributional conflicts, and the historical processes through which economies grew and declined."[17]

The persistence of the problem is highlighted in the recent resurgence of historical attention to these same topics, as seen in the NHC literature and parallel tracks. Yet the challenge we have witnessed is largely one of traditional historians who are steeped in contextual detail about economic events but ill-equipped to engage them with economic tools, hence Baptist's confusion-laden foray into national income accounting. The NHC literature at its worst accordingly becomes not a renewed exercise in qualitative economic history, but a somewhat haphazard misapplication of social history tools to the complex economic events of the past.

The resulting picture may seem mired in its inflexibility. On one side we find a self-limiting methodological rigidity that restricts its subject matter's accessibility to non-specialist audiences and self-limits the deployment of economic analysis to unconventional topics that are not easily quantified. On the other, we find a sea of abundant but cluttered detail and endless direction, yet also one where the only vessels are navigating by picking out bits and pieces of flotsam based on their resemblance to a strong and imported ideological prior that largely distrusts market capitalism itself.

Curiously, the classical liberal historian may be uniquely situated to operate across the rift in the history of capitalism. The conceptual toolbox of thinking economically—of grounding oneself in the concepts of scarcity, of trade-offs, of incentives, and of institutional political economy—provides an interpretive grounding that addresses the limitations of both sides. What might we find when we examine the effects of the institutional constraints of constitutions, the robustness of private property, and the conflict-adjudicating mechanisms of a legal system upon the economic events of the past? What happens when historical actors are scrutinized for their susceptibility to the same patterns of political economy that we witness among state actors in the present? How well do historical economic events since 1776 comport to or break from the original Smithian project of finding the underlying nature and causes of the wealth of nations? In short, a classical liberal approach to the history of capitalism might consider taking economic insights to topics that exist beyond the methodological barriers of cliometrics and yet are also neglected, or worse erroneously serviced, by historians who lack or even eschew and caricature economic intuition.

Slavery and Capitalism: Friend or Foe?

Despite enjoying a common and in some ways concurrent intellectual history with the emergence of capitalism, a classical liberal history of capitalism must also grapple with a related ailment of its subject's historical treatment that has become increasingly pronounced in recent years. Capitalism suffers from a definitional problem. While the persistence of market-hostile ideological frameworks in historical scholarship is in some ways a culprit, it is also the case that these new historians of "capitalism" simply lack a cohesive definition of the term and stumble from there into imprecision. The worst instances devolve into a dereliction of meaning itself, with the usage of the term "capitalism" taking on an almost intentionally pejorative character in the absence of anything more substantive.

A number of scholars have commented upon the pronounced "definitional elasticity" of recent historical work on capitalism, particularly within the NHC literature. Several NHC practitioners have in turn embraced this reluctance to define the term as a virtue of their approach. To quote NHC historian Seth Rockman, this line of study "has minimal investment in a fixed or theoretical definition of capitalism." Characterizing his approach as a process of inductive discovery, he openly concedes a willingness to let the term "float as a placeholder." Rockman further promotes a "capitalism" that is loosened from its conventional association with specific eras such as the industrial revolution, obviating questions of a pre-capitalist society or its causal role in transitions from an earlier state.[18] Louis Hyman echoes these sentiments even more forcefully in a recent *Journal of American History* roundtable on the subject: "Simply defining capitalism is a bad idea. It is too deductive."[19]

This curious state of affairs has received some pushback from other historians. In the same roundtable discussion, Scott Marler suggested this aversion to a definition was self-defeating in that it shirked an admittedly complex but historiographically important question. Tom Cutterham similarly criticized the "rather troubling" implications of Rockman's aversion to definitions precisely because they strip capitalism of its grounding in time. "If there was no transition to capitalism, if nothing can properly be called pre-capitalist, then has it simply always been here?" he asks. The result is to turn capitalism into an overly broad term, wherein it becomes impossible to "point to anything that was ever not capitalism."[20]

The NHC struggles with an adequate definition of capitalism create additional oddities, including contradicting its own claimed premise. Instead of inductively teasing out the historical mechanisms of capitalism, these definition-averse historians have created the conditions of a never-ending cycle of "discovering" something that is never quite fully revealed or specified.

Far more problematic though is a second and less-noticed implication of adopting an intentionally vague terminology. Even while claiming to eschew definitions of "capitalism," many of these same historians have in fact imported a certain semiotic fluidity to their deployment of the term. The result is not only to broaden its meaning, but to do so selectively and in ways that are vulnerable to the importation of intentionally disparaging characteristics.

Consider Rockman's example. In the very same sentence he touts the "disavowal of theoretical definitions" of capitalism as a necessary feature of its open inquiry, he announces quite confidently that NHC scholarship has shown "slavery as integral, rather than oppositional, to capitalism."[21] One cannot specify the characteristics of capitalism for even modest conceptual clarity, and yet slavery is already admitted as an integral characteristic of capitalism. A rather awkward doctrine, this!

Internally conflicted assessments of this type are not limited to Rockman. NHC historian Sven Beckert is even more brash in his assault on "capitalism's illiberal origins." At once evading a definition for capitalism and yet aggressively infusing it with specific—and damning—attributes, he pinpoints slavery as the "beating heart of this new system"—a system built not on property rights "but a wave of expropriation of labor and land."[22] Beckert too is quite certain that capitalism and slavery are not oppositional. Or as he approvingly paraphrases Walter Johnson's parallel argument in *River of Dark Dreams*, "slavery [is] not just as an integral part of American capitalism, but . . . its very essence."[23]

Issues of definitional rigor and consistency extend deep within the NHC literature, and Beckert offers his own addendum. By little more than reinventing terminology, he blends the attributes of 18th century imperial mercantilism —that aggressively managed symbiosis of economic interests and nationally minded state policies to drive expansion and industry—into market capitalism under the new moniker "war capitalism" and proceeds as if the two are unified, both in character and culpability for slavery and a host of other ills.[24] The pronounced adversarial tension that historically existed between market capitalism and the mercantile political agenda is almost entirely lost in the process, even as the past's participants in the intellectual contests between them would have balked at any attempt to blend the two together.

The abusiveness of the historical distortion exhibited in Beckert's move is no small point. It inverts the very premise of capitalism's most famous and influential exposition. Composed as a retort to the prevailing mercantilist economic theories of his day, Adam Smith's *Wealth of Nations* was also a far-reaching assault upon industrial protectionism in the name of national "wealth," upon public-private enterprises undertaken through the privileged arrangements of law and government access, upon militaristic imperialism and colonialism, and upon slavery itself.[25] Beckert's version of "capitalism," still wavering between a definition that is at once equivocal in its characteristics and yet selectively infused with the certitude of an "essence" chained to slavery, has effectively become the same horde of demons that the primary intellectual father of modern capitalism specifically contested and condemned in his seminal work.

Nor is Beckert anomalous in this practice. Johnson similarly invents the phrase "racial slave capitalism" to describe a program of white supremacist mercantile internationalism. The features of this "system" unite agriculture and industry around the steam transport of cotton through a vast and globally minded system of state collusion and a vigorously regulated color bar.[26] The resulting concoction is simultaneously part Friedrich List, part Henry Clay, part J. D. B. De Bow, and part George Fitzhugh, yet few of its ingredients are quintessentially capitalistic in the Smithian sense and many are explicitly antithetical. A large economic literature empirically establishes and expands upon the economic costs of a discriminatory legal regime, as well as the tendency of market forces to rub against statutorily entrenched racial codes.[27] Smith himself saw this tension at play in slavery, observing that the entire system was sustained upon the political assistance its beneficiaries afforded to themselves. Thus the slave owners "will never make any laws mitigating their usage; whatever laws are made with regard to slaves are intended to strengthen the authority of the masters and reduce the slaves to a more absolute subjection."[28]

This specific criticism is not offered to suggest that Smith retains a perpetual license upon determining the attributes of the economic system he described. Even the term's acquisition of its modern properties postdates his lifespan. Yet the pronounced dissimilarities between Smithian capitalism and what the NHC literature takes to be its subject matter point to another opportunity for classical liberal historians to unclutter the discussion. A history of capitalism attempted without the benefit of an intellectual history of capitalism arrives at strange and even self-contradictory positions, among them the odd state of affairs where capitalism becomes, by little more than a sleight of hand and twist in terminology, the very same practices of 18th-century political economy that Adam Smith and the other celebrated theorists of capitalism specifically argued against.

Anti-Capitalism as a Historical Method

There appears to be another twist at play in the definitional fluidity of the NHC, and it is here that the old Hayekian criticism's application to the modern literature becomes most salient. While selectively noncommittal phrasings and ahistorical inversions of terminology can serve as a mechanism to insulate a claim about the past from the sort of falsifiable testing that economic historians prefer, they also contrast with a consistent theme of the NHC genre found in its recurring portrayal of capitalism as an explicitly illiberal system, or one of uncontested illiberal byproducts. Beckert openly states as much in asserting the "illiberal origins" of modern market capitalism, and the larger NHC genre exhibits an almost singular preoccupation with forging a friendship between capitalism and slavery; and segregation; and colonialism; and exploitation, degradation, and violence, all chalked up to "market failure" or worse.[29] For all these attempts to forge—and force—an association between capitalism and a multitude of social wrongs and problems, a parallel neglect extends to the historical critics of capitalism as they saw the Smithian system unfolding in the world around them.

Seeing the now-disputed adversarial economic relationship between capitalism and slavery, many classical economists in the 18th and 19th centuries openly advanced abolitionist arguments in their works.[30] Less noticed as a historical point, however, is the frequency with which their contemporary advocates of economic regulation, of planned economic nationalism, and even slavery itself also perceived capitalism as a threat. A number of these anti-capitalist witnesses are noteworthy not only for their defenses of illiberal institutions and practices, but also as forbears of many of the same arguments against unchained markets—against the much-caricatured capitalist notion of laissez-faire—that persist to the present day.

Consider the case of Thomas Carlyle, the Scottish historian and social commentator who penned a now-notorious essay that blamed the economic decline of the British West Indies on emancipation. His 1849 lamentation took direct aim at what he famously dubbed the "dismal science"—a "rueful" enterprise "which finds the secret of this universe in 'supply and demand,' and reduces the duty of human governors to that of letting men alone," which is to say laissez-faire. To Carlyle, this new science of economy had joined itself to the "sacred cause of black emancipation, or the like, to fall in love and make a wedding of it" to yield "dark extensive moon-calves, unnameable abortions, wide-coiled monstrosities, such as the world has not seen hitherto."[31]

This bombastic slur was no passing criticism, but rather a sustained assault on market capitalism. Carlyle saw cause for alarm in the "multifarious devices we have been endeavoring to dispense with governing" in deference to markets where the two collided. He denounced the "superficial speculations, of laissez-faire, supply-and-demand" not only in its affinity for emancipation, but as a blamed cause for other ills of the day—for the Irish famine, as he extended his doctrines in the immediate wake of the 1849 essay.[32] In two decades' time, with abolition achieved not only in Britain's colonies but in the United States, he placed market capitalism at the center of blame for a society "fallen vulgar and chaotic" to the simultaneous forces of black equality and the "cheap and nasty"—his term for an over-commodified marketplace of unimpeded trade and what he saw as culturally degrading commercialism.[33]

A parallel witness may be seen in the previously referenced late antebellum theorist of the slaveocracy, George Fitzhugh. A self-described Carlylean, Fitzhugh was also an avowed anti-capitalist. Political economy, which "may be summed up in the phrase, 'Laissez-faire,' or 'Let alone'" was but a "false philosophy of the age."[34] These principles, he asserted in another text, "are at war with all kinds of slavery." Capitalism represented a competitive race to the bottom of wages in Fitzhugh's mind, and slavery was its well-ordered antithesis. Yet slavery was not Fitzhugh's only concern. He devoted chapters in both of his major works to lambasting the cause of free trade. Its intellectual champion Adam Smith was, to him, an "absent, secluded and unobservant" thinker who "saw only that prosperous and progressive portion of society whom liberty or free competition benefitted, and mistook its effects on them for its effects on the world." Just as revealing is Fitzhugh's antidote to this perceived state of affairs:[35]

> But [the South] does not let alone. She builds roads and canals, encourages education, endows schools and colleges, improves river navigation, excludes, or taxes heavily foreign show-men, foreign pedlars, sellers of clocks, etc. tries to build up by legislation Southern commerce, and by State legislation to multiply and encourage industrial pursuits. Protection by the State Government is her established policy—and that is the only expedient or constitutional protection. It is time for her to avow her change of policy and opinion, and to throw Adam Smith, Say, Ricardo & Co., in the fire.

Fitzhugh's political recommendation is, with no small irony, strikingly similar to the managerial mercantile platform that the NHC literature rebrands as "war capitalism" or "slave capitalism." Beckert offers a parallel rejection of "liberal, lean state" 19th-century Britain, depicting instead a slavery-fed plantation and cotton-driven "capitalist" empire with "a powerful and interventionist bureaucracy, high taxes, skyrocketing government debt, and protectionist tariffs," with "turnpikes and canals," and with conscious state policies to drive economic growth.[36] While the NHC literature diverges sharply from Fitzhugh in condemning the viciousness of slavery, its representation of the slave economy largely shares and emphasizes these same features: an assertion of the plantation system's economic prowess and dynamism, as distinct from classical economic criticisms that saw it as an inefficient and institutionally rigid throwback, and a mutual identification of slavery as the primary driving engine of economic industrialization taking place around it and in its wake. Fitzhugh also differs by including a more candid admission about his own adversaries. They are one and the same with the capitalist intellectuals that much of the NHC literature now carelessly lumps into an extension of Fitzhugh's slave-based economic system.

Anti-Capitalism and Progressive History

Carlyle's influence and reputation have diminished since his lifetime, and Fitzhugh was always considered something of a crank beyond the fire-eaters of the slave-owning political class. Parallel manifestations of anti-capitalism nonetheless transmitted into subsequent intellectual movements at the root of American progressivism.

To some degree, the modern roots of anti-capitalistic historical writing are products of intellectual histories about older theorists of capitalism. Richard Hofstadter's classic 1944 assault on the claimed "social Darwinism" of Herbert Spencer and other laissez-faire theorists of the late 19th century still looms large in the history profession's conceptualization of pre–progressive era models of capitalism. Hofstadter's text is not without flaws, as more recent works on Spencer have suggested, but neither is it without nuance. At points he takes a more progressive strain of "Darwinian collectivism" to task even as the thrust of his work targets the "individualist" varieties of laissez-faire capitalism.[37] A curious feature of the more recent historical literature is that it retains Hofstadter's disapproving depictions of Spencerian laissez-faire capitalism and inflates them to the point of caricature, placing them at the source of historical racism, exploitation theory, and most pre–welfare state social ills. At the same time though, a profound inattention may be observed in parallel treatments of progressive economic causes that resonate among anti-capitalists despite carrying profoundly illiberal racial and social baggage in their respective histories.

One noteworthy expression appeared among a group of politically progressive economists in the late 19th and early 20th century who consciously set out to supplant economic non-intervention with "scientific" correctives that aimed to alleviate a host of economic ills attributed to low wages and unemployment, distributional inequality, and regulatory laxity. This outwardly progressive counter to laissez-faire coalesced in the late 19th century around a group of economists and other social scientists who shared common intellectual roots, many of them having trained under the "younger" German Historical School at the Universities of Halle and Heidelberg. Though a new infusion to the classical-aligned American economics scene of the 1880s, these progressive reformers could trace their intellectual lineage back to the

60 | *The 1619 Project Myth*

older neo-mercantile political economy of Alexander Hamilton and its sub-sequent transmission to Germany in the early decades of the century.[38] The progressives used their academic work to advance a broad range of reformist causes, including labor unionization, work hour regulations, product safety regulations, anti-monopoly laws and trust-busting, "scientific" tariff targeting for strategic industries, redistributive taxation, and even the minimum wage. At the root of the movement was a widespread belief in the deployment of "scientific" managerial expertise to advise and design policies in areas where the unfettered free market fell short—where capitalism "failed" in their eyes.

The underlying rationale of progressive era economics is not far removed from similar progressive causes of today, including those championed by modern historian-advocates who are often drawn to these historical topics by political affinities and their own areas of interest. Indeed, the same NHC literature that condemns capitalism for an "integral" relationship with slavery a generation prior appears to hold the turn-of-the-century progressive rejoinder to laissez-faire in consistently high esteem. It entails a comparatively less developed body of work, though the thrust is highly approving of the progressive economic positions advanced by these historical figures.[39] Topically, there is little new to it save the investigation of unturned detail. The historiographical habit of portraying the progressive era as a corrective to the "excesses" of the Gilded Age is as old as it is oversimplified, yet it is also finding a comfortable embrace in recent NHC work.

The political economy of the progressive era warrants mention though for the complication it reveals, both historically among an identifiable group of capitalism's critics and in the present among historians who openly align with the causes they championed. Progressive scientism led its practitioners in a number of less-enlightened directions that are also just beginning to receive historical scrutiny. The product shows a selectivity of blame in the larger attempt to link capitalism to slavery's illiberal terms, juxtaposed against a polite inattention that sets in with issues that reflect poorly upon the liberality of progressive causes.

Classical liberal engagement with the history of capitalism should note the illiberal dimensions of progressivism in a growing body of recent work on the downsides of "scientific" planning. The same mindset that prompted the progressives to enlist state tools to counter the perceived "market failures" also saw, and for parallel rationales, an aggressive role for the state in the correction of other perceived social ills. Progressivism's faults extend directly into the realm of eugenics, of forced sterilization of the "unfit," and of an assortment of pseudo-scientific theories of racial biology and psychology. They include the use of minimum wage laws and work hour regulations to exclude black and immigrant laborers from the turn-of-the-century workforce. They include racially discriminatory and pseudo-scientific drug policies, the legacies of which persist in the prison system of our own time. They also show numerous instances where the segregationist strictures of Jim Crow found a welcome partnership not in capitalism, but among its critics and "reformers." Some of the figures are relatively obscure—Richard T. Ely, John R. Commons, and Simon N. Patten to name a few.[40] Others like Woodrow Wilson are well known for infusing progressivism into mainstream political economy into the present day, again on terms that sought to correct capitalism's claimed defects.

No less a source than John Maynard Keynes developed his original attack on market failure upon a eugenic argument for population controls. The "laissez-faire" of nature and heredity was, to him, as problematic as taking the same approach to an unregulated economic order.[41] While his and other progressive affinities for these causes dissipated among their heirs, their legacy as a matter of direct historical association with other more persistent causes remains politely overlooked—an oddly selective omission for a historical profession that has gone to extreme lengths to attach free market thinkers of the same era to a far flimsier affinity for social Darwinism.[42]

One possible counter for classical liberals is to investigate the little-studied resistance to scientific racism, eugenicism, and similarly blameworthy causes within the works of capitalism's historical defenders. Ludwig von Mises's answer to Keynes's eugenically tinged call for the "end of laissez-faire" is particularly revealing for its sounder positioning of the contesting causes of the day: "He who rejoices that peoples are turning away from liberalism, should not forget that war and revolution, misery and unemployment for the masses, tyranny and dictatorship are not accidental companions, but are necessary results of the anti-liberalism that now rules the world."[43]

These examples offer just a few cases in which pronounced strains of illiberalism have emerged among the historical critics of capitalism, both left and right. They offer an avenue of research in need of further exploration as a way of contextualizing history's capitalism as it was seen and lived by persons who charged it with varying degrees of defect. Their relevance to the current state of the field is further affirmed though in the comparative inattention their own ethical shortcomings have received within a NHC literature that is simultaneously all too eager to write faults into the core of the capitalist economic system—even where historical expositors of capitalism like Smith (or later figures such as Richard Cobden, J. E. Cairnes, and Edward Atkinson) specifically assailed the very same faults.

The Future of History and Capitalism

In offering these brief remarks on the emerging and still-fluid dimensions of the history of capitalism, much more remains unanswered about the trajectory of scholarship on this topic. Research within the NHC genre has grown in appeal and acclaim within the profession, yet its foundations, as noted, have many cracks in terms of how it engages the very concept of capitalism, how it defines its terminology, and the persistent issue of inattention to complicating evidence and methods from other lines of study. Moreover, the thrust of its message does not seem to be very far removed from the anti-capitalistic biases that Hayek diagnosed half a century ago, save for a marked increase in the intensity of expression. In some areas such as its treatment of slavery, the NHC literature has almost unwittingly revived a strain of anti-capitalistic arguments from the late antebellum itself and adapted them to historical analysis, minus of course the embrace of slavery.

Where this leaves the classical liberal historian of capitalism is in some ways dependent upon the topic being studied in an immensely broad field. But as a general principle I will suggest taking up the role of historical interlocutor through the joint tools of economic reasoning and evidentiary empiricism. Rather than offering a broad-based theory of capitalism, replete with claims of defined systems and normative judgments of what they should or should not achieve, a scrutinizing alternative might eschew the push to define "eras" of capitalism and its antecedents entirely. Rather, we might turn our analysis to simply discerning patterns of human choice amidst conditions of scarcity, subject to what we can discern from an evidentiary basis about the values and institutional constraints surrounding a past decision.

The search for a larger systemic narrative of the past may be an unavoidable encounter. But here too the search for the larger narrative's mechanisms can also function as its own test for the specific performance of these features, and recurring patterns that might be discerned from each. As a means of inquiry, we may make no promise that capitalism will perform as an ideal system and offer no claim of inoculation against past injustices, of which there are no shortage. Instead the classical liberal historian only seeks to understand them empirically as they are examined against the causal mechanisms of human exchange, both theorized and witnessed in similar circumstances of the past.

8

The New History of Capitalism Has a "Whiteness" Problem

In this piece, I look at some of the backlash against criticism of the 1619 Project by its editor Nikole Hannah-Jones and by some of its historian-defenders on Twitter. A common theme of the push-back has been to focus on the race, age, and gender of the project's historian-critics, including essentially dismissing them as "old white guys." Aside from the weakness of this line of argument as a means of eschewing substantive engagement, it suffers from another problem. The contested part of the 1619 Project does not pass its own test, as the NHC literature it heavily relies upon is almost exclusively written by a small and insular group of white scholars with Ivy League connections. The NHC literature is therefore susceptible to the same charge it makes against its critics.

THE NEW YORK TIMES'S 1619 Project is currently undergoing a new wave of scrutiny, spurred on—curiously enough—by the political left.[1] Over the course of the last month, an obscure socialist website landed interviews with Pulitzer Prize–winning historians James McPherson and Gordon Wood, as well as noted Civil War historian James Oakes, to solicit their opinions on the *Times*'s series.[2] The trio of historians pulled no punches while subjecting the project to scrutiny. Wood chastised its general thrust for diminishing the anti-slavery elements of the American Revolution, while Oakes and McPherson took issue with its reinterpretation of American capitalism as an outgrowth of plantation slavery.

66 | *The 1619 Project Myth*

Many of these observations echo my own criticisms of the project's misrepresentation of American economic history.[3] But the trio of scholars also offer significantly harsher assessments of the *Times*'s initiative on the whole.

On certain narrow points this involves pressing beyond the available evidence. For example, Oakes accuses 1619 Project editor Nikole Hannah-Jones of overstating Abraham Lincoln's support for the colonization of slaves abroad (echoing a line McPherson has also used in his other works by downplaying Lincoln's commitment to this policy).[4] This is a subject on which I possess more than a passing familiarity, and can say with certainty that Oakes and McPherson are in error.[5] The general criticisms from Oakes, McPherson, and Wood nonetheless reflect substantive and thoughtful engagement with the 1619 Project's narrative that—coming from distinguished sources—warrants a serious response.

It is therefore dismaying, although not surprising, to see McPherson, Wood, and Oakes being met with dismissive derision by many of the 1619 Project's defenders. "Is [Gordon Wood] under the illusion that the [*World Socialist Web Site* is] doing anything other than using him to club Black scholars?" asked Seth Rockman, a historian who was consulted on the 1619 Project's depiction of American capitalism.[6]

Similar comments from the history profession's younger generations pointed out that the critics were "old white males." Other academics, writing in this vein, accused them of excluding non-white and non-male scholars from their assessments of the materials involved—of effectively "liv[ing] in a silo" that refuses to engage "cutting edge" work by younger and minority scholars, as one historian put it.[7] If you've noticed a pattern here, recall how Ana Lucia Araujo, another NHC supporter, responded to me back in August 2019 when I began scrutinizing the 1619 Project's economic arguments.[8] This crowd often flees from substantive engagement over disputed scholarly claims, but they'll attack an interlocutor's race, gender, or age in a heartbeat.

Still, the neglect of a segment of the scholarly community is a potentially serious charge, even as these examples seem to service the objective of dismissing the 1619 Project's critics without actually engaging the substance of their criticisms. After all, a scholar's professional obligations include maintaining a familiarity with the latest research in his or her field when offering comments as an authority in that same field.

But is the charge even an accurate reflection of the debate over the 1619 Project?

I have to admit that I was somewhat taken aback to see this line of argument coming primarily from scholars who associate with the "New History of Capitalism" (NHC) school of thought, Rockman among them. The 1619 Project's editors relied almost entirely on NHC scholars for its treatment of slavery's economics, which appeared in a feature article by sociologist Matthew Desmond.[9] The dismissive attacks over race obscure additional fault with this editorial choice, as they set a standard that the NHC school itself does not meet.

Desmond's piece has become an acute point of contention for the project's critics, largely because he tries to weaponize the brutality of the plantation system to launch into a sweeping political attack on free market capitalism in the present day. This historical claim is fraught with errors of fact and evidence, yet its anti-capitalist ideology is also a dominant theme in several key works from the NHC genre—so dominant in fact that its claimed interest in the racial dimensions of history is largely subordinate to its economic interpretation.[10]

There's also a deeper irony at play though in the NHC backlash against McPherson, Wood, Oakes, and other 1619 Project critics. Far from representing non-white scholarly voices and introducing challenges to a previously stagnant historiography of slavery, the NHC school is actually a stunning embodiment of everything it charges against its critics.

We can see how by looking at Desmond's own article. By my count, Desmond interviewed seven current academic historians when framing his piece. All seven strongly associate with the NHC school. Several of its leading figures are among the consulted voices: Ed Baptist, Sven Beckert, Walter Johnson, Calvin Schermerhorn, and Rockman, as previously mentioned. Like Desmond himself, all seven of the consulted NHC historians are also white.

By contrast, the only black voices that speak in his piece at all are long-deceased scholars such as W. E. B. Du Bois. To the extent that the article even relies on academic literature, it comes almost entirely from books by the aforementioned scholars—all of them white.

While a historian's race (or gender or age) should not be used to determine the quality of his or her work, the deployment of this form of argument

68 | *The 1619 Project Myth*

against the 1619 Project's critics betrays a bizarre lack of self-awareness on the part of the NHC crowd. The modern NHC literature on capitalism and slavery contains very few, if any, non-white voices, and Desmond's article in the 1619 Project exemplifies this oversight. To borrow a little terminology from the critical theory–infused epistemology that this same school of historians often draws upon, it would appear that the New History of Capitalism has a "whiteness" problem.

The issues with the NHC complaints run deeper than its invoking of race to attack its critics though. These same scholars have made a habit of accusing their opponents of neglecting their own claimed insights to the history of slavery. That charge also runs strongly in the other direction. Despite their own self-promoted claims of "cutting edge" novelty, many of the NHC scholars actually inhabit an insular echo chamber of their own ideological compatriots.

These very same NHC scholars have attained notoriety in recent years for refusing to engage with or respond to academics in other disciplines who work on slavery, and even other historians who come from traditions outside the NHC ranks. Symptomatic of this insularity, the growing body of books and articles produced by NHC scholars often exhibit literature reviews that can only be described as ignorant or negligent of the past 50 years of scholarship on the subject, and particularly the work of economic historians.

Several academics from other branches of the slavery literature have documented this strange pattern of almost intentional disengagement from the rest of the literature by NHC historians. Economist Stanley Engerman pointed out as much in his review of the NHC genre.[11] He specifically singled out Ed Baptist, who cut off communications with his critics after his 2015 book *The Half Has Never Been Told* came under scrutiny by economists Alan Olmstead and Paul Rhode.[12] Baptist's silence includes a failure to correct or even address a major statistical error in his work, despite its continued repetition by other scholars and journalists.[13] As Engerman put it, Baptist's book contains "surprising omissions from the writings on slavery of the past half-century." He continues:

> Major descriptions of slave life by, for example, Kenneth Stampp
> (1956), Eugene Genovese (1974), and Ira Berlin (1998), are given
> brief (if any) mention. He does not fully engage at all in what

should be of major interest to him, the last decades of works concerning economic aspects of the slave economy by scholars such as Gavin Wright (2006), Roger Ransom and Richard Sutch (1977), and Claudia Goldin (1976), not to say Robert Fogel (1989) and Fogel and Engerman (1974), whose work is both drawn upon and harshly criticized elsewhere. These have been a major analytical and statistical battleground, but are not discussed in any detail. There is only some pre-emptory discussion towards the end of the book consistent with the recent outpouring of work on slave culture and agency, issues that some now consider central to understanding the lives of those enslaved.

Glaring literature review deficiencies of this sort extend to other works in the NHC genre. The late economic historian Richard Sutch noted similar oversights in a review essay of the economic literature, particularly as it concerned the voluminous scholarly debate precipitated by Engerman and Robert Fogel's landmark 1974 study *Time on the Cross*:[14]

> Recently two historians of American slavery, Sven Beckert and Seth Rockman, dismiss their own neglect with a single sentence. "The economic history of slavery has labored in the shadows of the interpretative controversies surrounding... *Time on the Cross*" [2016:10]. Presumably this excused them from critiquing the cliometric literature and freed them to contribute to and celebrate an alternative economic history of slavery and American economic development. Their loss (and ours) has become glaringly apparent in the recent discussion by cliometricians of what historians have come to call the "New History of Capitalism and Slavery."

In place of the necessary literature review, the NHC crowd frequently resorts to dismissiveness, derision, and ad hominem attacks. As Engerman reports, "the general response . . . by Baptist is to charge those who disagree with him, even when it is over what some might regard as 'merely' errors of historical fact and understanding, with racism." As the NHC backlash against more recent criticism of the 1619 Project reveals, the invoking of race for this purpose appears to be something of a default response.

This is a peculiar charge, as the main critics of the NHC literature make no arguments that could reasonably be described as racist. They in no way

70 | *The 1619 Project Myth*

deny the violent brutality of slavery. Nor do they downplay its horrors or economic scale, asking only that such assessments remain rooted in evidence. The NHC grievance, then, appears to consist of lashing out against scholars from other schools and other disciplines who find their own arguments wanting due to issues of historical accuracy and, in some cases, unambiguous empirical errors.

In a final stroke of irony, the same group of NHC scholars recently came under fire from an older historiographical tradition on the left for appropriating and misconstruing the work of its own leading scholars. In their effort to weaponize the history of slavery against modern capitalism, many NHC scholars have wrapped themselves in the mantle of Eric Williams, a black radical from the mid-20th-century Marxian tradition. His 1944 book *Capitalism and Slavery* is often invoked as a forerunner to today's NHC scholarship, though incorrectly so. Aside from the titular similarity, there's actually very little evidence that the NHC scholars engage with or meaningfully draw upon Williams's thesis. If anything, they cite it for its pairing of the words "capitalism" and "slavery" and then unintentionally invert its thesis.

Williams's most famous argument aimed to cast doubt upon conventional depictions of the abolitionist movement as a moral cause. Rather, he maintained that the rise of industrial capitalism rendered its earlier mercantile form obsolete, and with it undermined the Atlantic slave trade. The impetus for emancipation was thus a self-interested act of the capitalists, and still attached to colonial subjugation through their economic and political systems. Thus, whereas British industrial capitalism served as a self-interested agent of slavery's demise in Williams's telling, the NHC literature almost unwittingly flips the claim such that slavery becomes the mechanism of industrial capitalism's American ascendance.

Non-NHC scholars who come from Williams's school of thought, as well as traditional Marxists in general, are none too pleased at the "new" historians' appropriation. Indeed, the *World Socialist Web Site*'s eagerness to host interviews with McPherson, Wood, and Oakes likely reflects the website's operators attempts to position themselves as a contesting claimant to the history of slavery on the far left. While the deterministic economic arguments of the Williams thesis have not fared well in subsequent historical evaluation, they are historiographically important and, along with his mentor C. L. R.

James, form the basis of a Caribbean-centric black radical school of historical thought that is now in direct tension with the predominantly white and Ivy League-centric NHC school.[15]

Enter H. Reuben Neptune, a historian of the postcolonial Caribbean who comes from the same historiographical tradition as Williams and James. In a recent issue of the *Journal of the Early Republic,* Neptune painstakingly documents how several leading works in the NHC genre incorrectly invoke Williams as their own precursor while only engaging his text at a superficial level.[16] Beckert, Baptist, Johnson, and other NHC scholars thus end up "throwing scholarly shade" upon Williams's thesis, misrepresenting its purposes to their own ends.

Thus do we arrive at the unenviable position where scholars in the NHC genre are guilty of the very same faults that they invoke to dismiss critics of the 1619 Project. We arrive at a new historiographical body of scholars that operate in their own echo chamber, that misrepresent or completely neglect scholarly works from outside of that echo chamber, and that recklessly dismiss their critics on account of a racial demography that has an even more pronounced presence in their own ranks. Furthermore, in doing so, they lay mistaken claim to a competing black radical historiographic tradition, essentially botching its most famous arguments in the process through a careless and politicized reading.

The *Times*'s 1619 Project remains an evolving work, and its other contributions extend beyond the current debate over its treatment of slavery and capitalism. But notice that the project's studies of the 20th and 21st centuries have attracted far less controversy than the Desmond article or the slavery and capitalism debate.

That debate is a flashpoint for criticism precisely because of its overreliance on the flawed New History of Capitalism school. Until its authors and editors recognize this skew and substantively engage with the deep factual and historiographical problems that afflict this literature, they can expect to face similar criticisms from the broader scholarly world outside of the NHC genre.

9

What the 1619 Project's Critics Get Wrong About Lincoln

While many assessments of the 1619 Project have raised the need for significant factual corrections to its historical narrative, one area where a large number of historians go astray is its treatment of Abraham Lincoln. The 1619 Project correctly called attention to the complexities of Lincoln's own thoughts about race in a post-emancipation society, noting the tension caused by his lifelong interest in the voluntary but subsidized colonization of African-Americans abroad. Colonization makes for a lively subject of interpretive debate around Lincoln, but several prominent critics have adopted a stance that either downplays or denies the significance of this concept to Lincoln's racial beliefs.

By happenstance this aspect of Lincoln's life and presidency falls squarely in my own published research area dating back over a decade, encompassing multiple scholarly articles and a 2011 monograph on the subject. The Times's *project lead Nikole Hannah-Jones even cited my work to rebut early criticisms of her treatment of Lincoln before realizing it came from a critic of other essays in the series. Nonetheless, credit is due on this specific point and, in the interest of factual accuracy, I draw upon that research to document the many ways in which other 1619 Project detractors get Lincoln wrong.*

SINCE ITS PUBLICATION last August, the *New York Times's* 1619 Project has come under a barrage of withering critiques. Historians took it to task for exaggerating the role of slavery as a motivating factor behind the Revolutionary War, while economists quickly dissected its empirically

74 | *The 1619 Project Myth*

suspect attempt to redefine modern American capitalism as an outgrowth of the "King Cotton" plantation economies of the antebellum period.

In its worst instances, the 1619 Project amounts to an unscholarly mess of historical misrepresentations, economic fallacy, and an explicit anti-capitalist ideological agenda. To the project's further discredit, the *Times*'s editors and main contributors have adopted a dismissive stance in response to substantive criticism, including a refusal to correct documented factual errors[1] among its historical claims.

Not all criticisms of the *Times*'s initiative have hit their mark though.

Consider the case of Abraham Lincoln, whose support for the colonization of former slaves in tropical locales outside of the United States came under the scrutiny of project organizer Nikole Hannah-Jones. In a speech before a group of free African-Americans at the White House on August 14, 1862, Lincoln observed, "Without the institution of slavery and the colored race as a basis, the war could not have an existence." Given the likely persistence of racial conflict, he concluded, "It is better for us both, therefore, to be separated."

Hannah-Jones uses this lesser-known example of Lincoln's politics to impart complexity to his reputation as a racial egalitarian, including hints that the "Great Emancipator" exhibited misgivings over the prospect of political equality in the post-slavery United States. Several of the most effective critics of the project's faulty Revolutionary War thesis then pounced on this Civil War–era suggestion as an example of another error.

Allen Guelzo, a prominent conservative historian, dubs the characterization an "outrageous, lying slander" against Lincoln, while Sean Wilentz, a noted progressive scholar, charges that Hannah-Jones had used the issue to obscure Lincoln's larger aim of advancing emancipation, unattached to any colonization proviso.[2]

In both historians' accounts, Lincoln's interest in colonization is relegated to its limited deployment as a temporary political tool, and possibly insincerely at that, after which it could be discarded from the emancipation story.

Wilentz achieves this dismissal by erroneously reporting that Lincoln decoupled colonization from his preliminary Emancipation Proclamation of September 1862.[3] This document's second paragraph actually announced the continuation of the government's "effort to colonize persons of African descent, with their consent." He then further excises the policy from the District of Columbia Emancipation Act, which actually contained $100,000 in colonization funding—reportedly the main factor that induced Lincoln to sign the measure.[4]

Guelzo goes even further, recasting colonization as something of a political ruse by Lincoln to lull the Northern electorate into accepting the more radical proposition of abolishing slavery. Or as he puts it, colonization was "the great tranquilizer of white anxiety" during the months leading up to the Emancipation Proclamation. Such speculations are not new. They date to the Civil War era itself, and Guelzo quotes one such example in the journalist Frederick Milnes Edge, who pondered from afar that the aforementioned D.C. Emancipation Act's colonization fund had been promoted by Lincoln "to silence the weak-nerved."

Though it was unknown to Edge as he penned these words and, apparently, Guelzo today, Lincoln's own actions in the wake of the D.C. Emancipation Act contradict this suggestion. On the day after he signed the measure, Lincoln secretly summoned the African-American abolitionist and Liberian missionary Alexander Crummell to the White House for an informal conversation about soliciting recruits to use the measure's colonization provisions.[5]

Edge's speculative explanation for Lincoln's many public colonization remarks has nonetheless proven a powerful intoxicant for historians who desire an exonerative explanation for their content. Thus writers such as Guelzo and Wilentz echo it today, and advance an account of Lincoln almost wholly divorced from his colonization arguments. With palliative deed complete and the tranquilizer serving its political purpose, Lincoln then supposedly abandoned the proposal and "sloughed off" colonization for good, to use an oft-quoted line from the diary of his secretary John Hay.

Both views are steeped in an older literature of Lincoln biography and commentary, including the two authors' own work. But as we shall see, that same literature is almost 20 years out of date, having missed several subsequent archival discoveries that belie its contentions.[6]

The first complicating factor is a succession of previously unknown records in foreign repositories revealing long-lost efforts of the Lincoln administration

76 | *The 1619 Project Myth*

to secure prospective colonization sites from foreign governments.[7] With materials in the government archives of the United Kingdom, the Netherlands, Belize, Jamaica, and Denmark, these records attest to a shift in Lincoln's colonization policies that began around January 1863.

Having encountered the plagues of public graft and corruption in his earlier colonization ventures with private landholders, Lincoln turned to the secretive channels of diplomacy and what were seen as stable European powers with labor-starved Caribbean colonies. In sum, these State Department initiatives extend the known record of Lincoln's colonization program over a year beyond the final Emancipation Proclamation of January 1, 1863.

Second, and contrary to the suggestions of both Wilentz and Guelzo, Lincoln clearly envisioned colonization as a corollary policy to the more famous Proclamation. While Guelzo and Wilentz demarcate January 1, 1863, as the end of Lincoln's colonization interests, the 16th president actually spent the evening before his most famous act in the company of colonization negotiators. They were putting the finishing touches on a pilot program to transport some 500 freed slaves from Fort Monroe, Virginia, to a prospective colony on the Île-à-Vache off the coast of Haiti. The project's agent, Bernard Kock, returned to the White House in the company of Sen. James R. Doolittle the next day to obtain the president's signature on the finalized arrangement only an hour before he issued his more famous Proclamation.

Although the details of Kock's contract were intentionally obscured from the press so as to avoid the political corruption that plagued an earlier and more public colonization project the previous fall, Lincoln actually signaled his intention for emancipation and colonization to proceed hand-in-hand.[8] The day after the Proclamation, an anonymous editorial appeared in the *Washington Morning Chronicle* announcing its consummation as "initial point of separation of the black from the white race" through voluntary colonization abroad. The article's hidden author was John Nicolay, the president's personal secretary.

Lincoln, for his own part, pitched the scheme out of a genuine concern that the post-slavery South would devolve into institutionalized racial terrorism at the hands of former plantation owners. This pessimistic appeal earned him the ire of Frederick Douglass, who denounced him as an "itinerant colonization preacher." But his scheme also resonated with other black abolitionists including Henry Highland Garnet, a leader of New York City's black community who barely escaped the violence of a white-supremacist mob during the New York Draft Riots of 1863, and John Willis Menard, who later became the first African-American to win election to Congress. In fact, the 1862 White House speech highlighted in Hannah-Jones's essay entailed one such attempt to sway a free black audience into accepting colonization as a safety valve from racial oppression in a post-slavery South.

Both the Haitian venture and the arrangements with the European powers would falter over the next year, though not for want of Lincoln's own recurring efforts to breathe life into them. As the president explained to a British visitor in June 1863, colonization was his "honest desire." Lincoln nonetheless found his "colonization hobby," as he often referred to it, hamstrung by political setbacks.

William Seward, Lincoln's otherwise-loyal secretary of state, opposed the project and settled into a pattern of intentionally dragging his feet when processing the president's colonization directives.[9] At one point in August 1863, Lincoln had to personally order Seward to transmit a signed colonization agreement to the British legation in Washington, D.C., after the secretary had sat upon it for almost two months. That same November, Seward stalled a signed colonization treaty between the United States and the Netherlands by declining to submit it to the Senate for ratification.[10]

A series of mishaps plagued the Île-à-Vache project, beginning with a smallpox outbreak shortly after the expedition set sail in April 1863 and culminating almost a year later when the colony collapsed from mismanagement and had to be rescued by the U.S. Navy. The publicity surrounding the disaster and the political bickering it provoked as competing government officials rushed to point fingers of blame further dampened congressional enthusiasm for continuing the president's colonization programs.

Finally, the persistent presence of political graft caught Congress's attention during an annual review of approximately $600,000 in dedicated colonization funding in 1864. After discovering financial improprieties implicating a cabinet official and suggesting that a sitting U.S. senator had absconded with several thousand dollars from the account, legislators moved to rescind the appropriation in June 1864. This event prompted Hay's aforementioned diary entry that the president had "sloughed off" colonization, but neither Guelzo nor Wilentz supply the context of Hay's next passage:

> Mitchell says Usher allows Pomeroy to have the records of the Chiriqui matters away from the Department to cook up his fraudulent accounts by. If so, Usher ought to be hamstrung.

John Palmer Usher was the secretary of the interior, accused of permitting illicit access to the colonization account. Samuel Pomeroy was the implicated senator, having previously held a contract on a competing colonization project in modern-day Panama. Perhaps most importantly, Hay's named source for this information was James Mitchell, a longtime Lincoln associate who now served as the government's colonization commissioner.[11]

Far from signaling the abandonment of the program, Hay's passage reveals that Mitchell was whistleblowing to the White House about corruption in the program. Mitchell himself would later record a conversation with the president from the same week. Lincoln informed his colonization commissioner that the recent congressional action constituted an "unfriendly" amendment to the budget. Lincoln, it now appears, had not experienced the change of heart that Guelzo and Wilentz imply from Hay's comment. Rather, he was angry that his subordinates were stealing money from the colonization account and frustrated by Congress's decision to strip away the funding.

While this setback effectively iced the remaining colonization initiatives of the administration for the duration of the Civil War, there are several signs that Lincoln intended to revive the program after the resumption of peace. After his reelection in November 1864, Lincoln moved to replace Usher in his cabinet with James Harlan, a colonization supporter and close friend of Mitchell. Lincoln also solicited his attorney general, Edward Bates, for a legal opinion that would allow him to sustain a small budget and back pay for Mitchell's office, in lieu of the suspended funding.

The final clue came on February 1, 1865, in the form of a recently discovered memorandum. Mitchell apparently met that morning with Rep. Thaddeus Stevens, the powerful chairman of the House Ways and Means Committee, to discuss a proposal that would see the colonization office's funding partially restored as the war wound to an end.[12] Stevens, who had shepherded the 13th Amendment through the House of Representatives only a day earlier, appended his signature on the memorandum for intended delivery to the president. His accompanying note read simply, "I cheerfully recommend the above named settlement."

Lincoln either never received Stevens's note, or never had the opportunity to act upon it, as he fell to an assassin's bullet on the evening of April 14, 1865. The question of what, if any, role colonization might have come to play in the racial policies of Lincoln's second term is therefore necessarily unanswerable, although Capitol Hill chatter from the early spring of 1865 hinted that Lincoln intended to appoint Mitchell to an unspecified role in the newly created Freedmen's Bureau. The former colonization commissioner's files at the National Archives contain a long list of senators' signatures on a statement endorsing this proposed transfer of roles.

What we do know for certain is how Lincoln's own friends and associates understood his position on colonization in his lifetime, as several left testimonials on the subject that chafe with the two historians' assessments. Note that Guelzo, in another critical essay on the 1619 Project, characterized the 16th president's position thusly: "Lincoln was, at best, ambivalent about colonization."[13]

Contrast this dismissive assessment with the words of William Seward, conveyed to a bedside visitor during his own long recovery from a parallel assassination attempt on the night of John Wilkes Booth's infamous deed:

> "No knife was ever sharp enough to divide us upon any question
> of public policy," said the Secretary, "though we frequently came
> to the same conclusion through different processes of thought."
> "Only once," he continued musingly, "did we disagree in senti-
> ment . . . His colonization scheme."

As we grapple with the substantive historical defects of the 1619 Project —and there are many—it is important to do so from a position of rigorous adherence to historical evidence. It is also important to temper our temptation to overinterpret the same evidence from the vantage point of the present. While Lincoln's colonization remarks grate the modern ear, and evince a patronizing paternalism toward the program's intended participants, they also reflect the sincerity of his anti-slavery beliefs and an accompanying recognition that white-supremacist violence would not end with the formal abolition of the institution.

This condition need not be gratuitously vilified, as the 1619 Project risks doing in the absence of temperate analysis, but nor should it be obscured with misleading and mistaken historical arguments offered for the sake of discrediting a point where the 1619 Project actually has the stronger case.

Instead we might ponder why the assessments of Wilentz and Guelzo veer so far from the evidentiary record, encompassing not only new archival discoveries but also common knowledge in Lincoln's own lifetime. One eyewitness to the emancipation story left a final clue to the complexities of Lincoln's thought.

While recording his own memories after the war, Lincoln's secretary of the Navy, Gideon Welles, recounted Lincoln's simultaneous pursuit of emancipation and colonization. They "were, in his mind, indispensably and indissolubly connected."

10

The 1619 Project: An Epitaph

Over the course of the 1619 Project roll-out and debate, the Times's *interactions with its scholarly critics became increasingly strained and dismissive. I experienced this rebuff directly in my efforts to prompt a correction to Matthew Desmond's essay on slavery and capitalism, but the most intense dispute involved the project's reimagining of the American Revolution as an effort to protect and preserve slavery from a posited but weakly attested British shift toward emancipation. A little over seven months after the project first appeared in print, one of its own consulted fact-checkers broke her silence and revealed that she had cautioned the paper against pushing this thesis—only to be ignored. In this essay I discuss the development, along with an intentionally understated but revealing correction that it prompted from the newspaper. When contextualized amid the larger debate, this embarrassing incident reveals the ideological nature of the 1619 Project and how the* Times's *prioritization of its political message has harmed and largely discredited its once-promising value as a work of historical interpretation.*

IT TOOK SIX months of heated debate to reach this point, but the *New York Times*'s 1619 Project has finally offered a small but crucial concession to its critics. On March 11, the paper published an "update" to indicate that it would be changing a disputed line of text in the lead essay by Nikole Hannah-Jones.[1] The change concerns one of the more visible points of contention from the preceding months.

As originally framed, the 1619 Project depicted the preservation of slavery against a British emancipatory threat as a central motivating factor for the American Revolution. They are now relaxing that claim to suggest that preserving slavery was a motive for only *some of* the colonists."

The *Times*'s correction comes across as a minor edit on paper, but behind those two altered words is a stunning concession. Over the previous six months, Hannah-Jones maintained an unyielding hold to her original essay's claim, and did so under intense scrutiny from experts on the subject. The assignment of primacy to slavery as a revolutionary cause became a focal point of a letter by five leading historians to the *Times* calling on the paper to issue a correction, which prompted a dismissive reaction back in December from both Hannah-Jones and the magazine's editor, Jake Silverstein.[2]

Much of the contention focused upon a late 1775 attempt by Lord Dunmore, the British governor of Virginia, who moved to preserve his rule by drawing the slaves of rebellious colonists into his militia in exchange for their freedom.

The Dunmore Proclamation revealed one of the many ways in which slavery cut across the other dividing lines of the revolutionary period, but it did not portend a coming general emancipation from the Crown.[3] Indeed, most slave-owning colonists perceived the measure as an attempt to incite a slave revolt against opponents of the British rule, rather than a sign of slavery's weakening position. The proclamation conveniently exempted the slaves of loyalist plantation owners, and Dunmore himself left a sordid record as supporter and beneficiary of slavery in the British colonial system. Meanwhile, as the long fight to abolish the institution made all too clear, supporters of slavery maintained firm majorities in the British Parliament at the time—and would continue in power for several decades to come.

Most of the problems with this key point in the 1619 Project's narrative appear to have stemmed from the way that Hannah-Jones went about researching and preparing her collection of essays. While the *New York Times Magazine* feature emerged under the consultation of several expert scholars in other areas of the 400-year swath of American history under its scope, it used very few specialists in the period between the American Revolution and the Civil War—arguably the most crucial period for the study of slavery in the United States.

Instead, Hannah-Jones took on this subject herself or assigned specific themes from this period to non-experts, such as Princeton sociologist Matthew Desmond, who wrote an accompanying piece on the economics of slavery despite having no scholarly competencies in that subject.

The results have made the period of 1775 to 1865 an acute vulnerability for the 1619 Project, even as the remainder of the initiative has faced far less criticism. At this point it would be accurate to conclude that the reputation of the project's other essays, many of them entirely unobjectionable adaptations of scholarly insights for a popular audience, has suffered because of the *Times*'s inflexible refusal to address erroneous historical claims in the essays by Hannah-Jones and Desmond.

When specialists in the 1775–1865 period began to scrutinize the *Times*'s claims about this period, they quickly identified multiple glaring errors of fact and interpretation alike. Hannah-Jones had grossly exaggerated the Dunmore Proclamation and misinterpreted its political ramifications to the revolution, ahistorically recasting the British as something of an existential threat to American slavery. In similar fashion, Desmond botched several basic facts about the economic history of slavery.[4] He severely overstated the economic significance of cotton to industrialization, while also misreading and misrepresenting evidence he enlisted to argue that the plantation economy stains and discredits modern American capitalism.[5]

While the *Times* has thus far evaded scrutiny of Desmond's claims, Hannah-Jones began casting about after the fact for scholars who would lend credence to her elevation of slavery to preeminence among the motives behind the Declaration of Independence.

In time she was able to cherry-pick an eclectic literature from a handful of historians that assign more emphasis to the effects of Dunmore's act on the revolutionary cause. However, as Cathy Young documents, most of these scholars assert much more tempered variants of this thesis under heavy qualifiers that were absent from Hannah-Jones's own depiction, and the few who do not offer arguments that collapse under evidentiary scrutiny.[6]

At the same time, Hannah-Jones's own response to her scholarly critics devolved from an initial respectful engagement to aggressive derision. She attacked the scholarly credentials of James McPherson and Gordon Wood, two of the most famous historians to question her narrative.[7] In one perplexing tweet, she singled out the critics as "white historians" (oddly neglecting the lack of racial diversity among the scholars who advised Desmond's own 1619 Project contribution).[8] When a group of conservative African-American academics and journalists launched a competing "1776 Project" in early 2020 to offer a counter-narrative, Hannah-Jones bombarded them with a string of personal attacks, the gist of which amounted to declaring them unworthy of her attention.[9]

From Silverstein's rebuff of the essay's historian critics to Hannah-Jones's dismissive and insulting demeanor, the message was clear.[10] The *Times* would not be amending its content, even to account for substantive evidence-based criticism of its factual and interpretive mistakes. This inflexible stance even extended to clearly documented errors, such as Hannah-Jones's misuse of the Dunmore proclamation. When I directed Silverstein to a line in Desmond's essay that specifically contradicted its own cited source by imparting a slavery-based origin story to modern Microsoft Excel spreadsheets, he similarly declined to offer any correction or clarification.[11] The paper's commitment to its published claims remained inflexible, no matter the error. Scholarly assessments of the project itself were unwelcome, unless they offered support to the 1619 Project's preexisting narrative.

So what brought about the *Times*'s sudden, if underplayed, reversal?

On March 6, 2020, *Politico* published a surprise essay by historian Leslie M. Harris that upended the 1619 Project debate.[12] Although its author chided some of the historian-critics of the project for allegedly understating slavery in their own work, she also had a stunning revelation about Hannah-Jones's essay.

The previous summer Harris had been contacted by the *Times* to serve as a fact-checker on the 1619 Project's discussions of slavery, one of her areas of specialization. The newspaper had asked her to verify the following claim:

> One critical reason that the colonists declared their independence from Britain was because they wanted to protect the institution of slavery in the colonies, which had produced tremendous wealth. At the time there were growing calls to abolish slavery throughout the British Empire, which would have badly damaged the economies of colonies in both North and South.

In Harris's own words, "I vigorously disputed the claim. Although slavery was certainly an issue in the American Revolution, the protection of slavery was not one of the main reasons the 13 Colonies went to war." The *Times*'s editors ignored her warning and ran with Hannah-Jones's argument anyway.

It took less than a week for the *Times* to migrate from its previous steadfast defense of the claim to the concession noted at the outset of this essay. Even then, the concession remains understated.

The newspaper's peculiar wording attempted to chalk the confusion up to interpretive ambiguities by its readers. In Silverstein's words, the *Times* recognized "that our original language could be read to suggest that protecting slavery was a primary motivation for all of the colonists. The passage has been changed to make clear that this was a primary motivation for some of the colonists."

Contrast that with the original passage, which stated, "Conveniently left out of our Founding mythology is the fact that one of the primary reasons the colonists decided to declare their independence from Britain was because they wanted to protect the institution of slavery."

There is no issue where the passage "could be read to suggest" an erroneous historical claim. It made that claim outright in unambiguous language that Hannah-Jones subsequently doubled down upon and, until the correction, showed few signs of ever relaxing or qualifying.

Still, the concession revealed more than its guarded conciliatory language displayed. Although they are conspicuously unacknowledged in Silverstein's correction note, the critics of the 1619 Project were on solid ground to question this claim and did so when it first appeared in print over six months earlier. The *Times*, in turn, behaved atrociously in deflecting and denying a substantive scholarly challenge to its content until its hand was forced.

Thus we are left with "could be read to suggest." That tepid backtracking, in effect, gave away the game. It's a fitting epitaph to what could have been an important and provocative contribution to historical inquiry about the lasting harms of slavery in the United States, but instead veered down the path of an ideological project, consumed by maintaining its own 21st-century political narrative above the history it weaponized to that cause.

II

Should K–12 Classrooms Teach from the 1619 Project?

As the political debate over the 1619 Project intensified before the 2020 presidential election, I began to receive inquiries about the suitability of its content for K–12 classroom adoption. I favored and still support instruction that teaches the debate concerning the 1619 Project, provided that it includes a balanced perspective featuring the many substantive criticisms of the project's claims and content. The New York Times *has shown no reciprocal interest in such a debate, however. Instead, the newspaper has aggressively pushed a one-sided curriculum based on the 1619 Project and launched at its inception through the Pulitzer Center.*

In this essay, I evaluate the merits of the newspaper's push to adopt the 1619 Project in public school classrooms. The newspaper's own vacillation about the primary purpose of its endeavor—Is it scholarly history or opinion writing?—presents complications for its curricular adoption, while also explaining some of the project's shortcomings. In the end, I trace the problems with the 1619 Project to the substandard scholarly qualifications of the authors chosen to directly address slavery in the period between the American Revolution and the Civil War.

This crucial period of 1776 to 1865 includes the most problematic essays in the 1619 Project, none of which were written by subject matter experts. Instead, project creator Nikole Hannah-Jones assigned these tasks to opinion journalists (including herself), explaining the unfamiliarity with the scholarly literature that is visible in the project's essays about this period. The result is a mismatch between the

88 | *The 1619 Project Myth*

> Times's *attempts to claim scholarly credibility and content in the 1619 Project that falls short of this self-depiction. When evaluated for its scholarly characteristics in the affected sections, the 1619 Project curriculum falls far short of any reasonable standard of classroom adoption.*

THE NEW YORK TIMES'S 1619 Project has come under renewed scrutiny as the latest flashpoint in the heated cultural battles over education policy. Since its inception, the *Times,* through a partnership with the Pulitzer Center, has aggressively pushed state and local school boards to adopt its controversial readings about slavery and American history as part of their K–12 school curricula.[1] All the while, the "newspaper of record" has adamantly refused to address the factual errors that plague several of the 1619 Project's feature essays and render it unsuitable for classroom instruction. In a blusterous string of tweets before the 2020 election, President Donald Trump recently answered the newspaper's campaign by threatening to suspend federal funding for public schools that adopt the curriculum.

Although the bickering between the *Times* and Trump had more to do with political posturing than substantive policy outcomes, it nonetheless raised an important question about the newspaper's aims with its classroom adoption campaign. Is the 1619 Project a substantive reenvisioning of American history, built upon rigorous scholarly analysis of the past? Or is it simply editorial journalism, intended to advance the *Times*'s political positions in the present day?

Unfortunately, 1619 Project creator Nikole Hannah-Jones has cluttered the discussion by purposefully invoking both claims as a matter of convenience. She originally marketed the product as "a history that you can easily use to discuss with your children" and a reenvisioning of educational content around slavery to ensure "we do not have to reteach this history in the future because we have taught it to our children right in the first place."[2] When facing scrutiny over specific deficiencies in its historical claims, however, Hannah-Jones makes a hasty retreat for the cover provided by its journalism origins.

The product is something of a Schrödinger's 1619 Project: it is simultaneously a contribution to historical scholarship when academic branding helps to lend credibility to its classroom adoption, and yet it is also just opinion journalism when its historical claims are subjected to scrutiny and found wanting.

The distinction matters greatly, as advocacy journalism is held to much lower standards of accuracy than scholarship, and intentionally blends factual content with normative propositions aimed at espousing a favored political stance. To use an analogy, it's the difference between teaching an introductory economics class from Paul Krugman's bestselling undergraduate textbook *Economics* and teaching the same class by assigning a selectively curated list of Krugman's weekly political columns for the *New York Times*.[3]

At this point it is probably safe to conclude that the 1619 Project fits squarely in the realm of advocacy journalism. Hannah-Jones has been candid about this aim when it suits her, including an admission that the project seeks to build support for the enactment of a slavery reparations program in the present day.[4] Although some of the 1619 Project's less controversial essays reflect popular distillations of their authors' academic work, these shorter vignettes have not attracted the level of criticism surrounding the project's feature essays over their explicitly political messages. Indeed, the overwhelming focus of critical scrutiny centers upon just two contributions to the 1619 Project: the lead essay by Hannah-Jones herself, particularly concerning its problematic claims about the American Revolution, and an error-riddled, retraction-worthy essay by sociologist Matthew Desmond on the economics of slavery.

As scrutiny mounted over the contributions of Hannah-Jones and Desmond, ultimately rendering several of their claims untenable, the *Times* itself doubled down into a position of outright incorrigibility. After six months of intense criticism and a surprise revelation that the paper ignored its own fact-checker, *Times* magazine editor Jake Silverstein published a tepid single-line backtrack of its historically unsupported characterization of slavery as a primary impetus for the American Revolution.[5] To date, the paper has not published a single word acknowledging the many problems with Desmond's essay, including his direct misrepresentation of recent empirical findings on the causes of the cotton economy's growth before the Civil War.

Nonetheless, Hannah-Jones has adopted another tactic to insulate these two essays from scrutiny. When pressed on their specific shortcomings, the *Times* reporter now retreats to the academic résumés of a handful of its

Ivy League contributors to lend the entire product scholarly legitimacy. "Had you actually read the 1619 Project, which you clearly haven't, you'd know historians with PhDs from Princeton and Harvard wrote for the project," she tweeted in 2020.[6]

It's a claim that she's repeated dozens of times over.

Hannah-Jones's invoking of scholarly prestige amounts to a deeply misleading characterization of the 1619 Project's content.

Two Ivy League historians, Harvard's Khalil Gibran Muhammad and Princeton's Kevin M. Kruse, did in fact write feature essays for the 1619 Project. But neither Muhammad nor Kruse's contributions pertained to claims or the historical period at the center of the 1619 Project controversies. Muhammad and Kruse are both specialists in 20th-century topics such as the civil rights movement and the history of race relations. Their two essays for the *Times* reflected this expertise, and attracted little controversy.

Yet neither Muhammad nor Kruse's résumés are sufficient to provide cover to the 1619 Project's contested material, including the crucial period between 1775 and 1865 where slavery was the central focus of its narrative. These bookends encompass the years between the start of the American Revolution and the end of the Civil War—arguably the most important period in American history for understanding the political development, entrenchment, and eventual destruction of the slave system.

Instead of using scholars who focus on this crucial period to inform the 1619 Project's narrative on slavery, Hannah-Jones assigned it to journalists such as herself and fellow *New York Times* writer Jamelle Bouie, or to nonspecialists such as Desmond, who had no prior academic expertise on the subject of 19th-century slavery let alone its complex economic dimensions.

A breakdown of the 1619 Project's 12 main feature contributions reveals the full severity of this problem.

Of the 12 main features, 6 were written by journalists including four in-house writers from the *Times*. One is a photographic essay, another is an assortment of literary contributions written by English and poetry professors, and a third is a legal analysis of prison reform policy—all ostensibly worthwhile contributions, but not the subject of focus for the ensuing controversy over the 1619 Project. The two historians' contributions, as noted, come from 20th-century specialists. Indeed, the only 19th-century historian the 1619 Proj-

Title	Scope	Author(s)	Author's Profession
America Wasn't a Democracy Until Black Americans Made It One	Slavery in 17th–19th centuries, American Revolution	Nikole Hannah-Jones	Journalist – *New York Times*
American Capitalism Is Brutal. You Can Trace That to the Plantation	Economics of slavery in 19th century	Matthew Desmond	Sociologist, 20th-century race relations – Princeton
A New Literary Timeline of African-American History	Literature	Various – 16 different writers	English and poetry professors, film directors, fiction writers
How False Beliefs in Physical Racial Difference Still Live in Medicine Today	History of race in medicine	Linda Villarosa	Journalist – *Essence* magazine
What the Reactionary Politics of 2019 Owe to the Politics of Slavery	Slavery in the early United States, 21st-century politics	Jamelle Bouie	Journalist – *New York Times*
Why Is Everyone Always Stealing Black Music?	History of music	Wesley Morris	Journalist – *New York Times*
How Segregation Caused Your Traffic Jam	History of urban/suburban development	Kevin Kruse	Historian, 20th-century race relations – Princeton
Why Doesn't America Have Universal Healthcare? One Word: Race	Health care policy	Jeneen Interlandi	Journalist – *New York Times*
Why American Prisons Owe Their Cruelty to Slavery	Prison reform policy	Bryan Stevenson	Attorney
The Barbaric History of Sugar in America	History of sugar production	Khalil Gibran Muhammad	Historian, 20th-century race relations – Harvard
How America's Vast Racial Wealth Gap Grew: By Plunder	Racial wealth gap in the US from post–Civil War to present day	Trymaine Lee	Journalist – MSNBC
Their Ancestors Were Enslaved by Law. Now They're Lawyers	Photo essay	Djeneba Aduayom	Photographer (with text and layout provided by *New York Times* staff)

92 | *The 1619 Project Myth*

ect used, Tiya Miles, did not contribute a feature article but rather a series of short vignettes about slavery's role in migration and agriculture. These mini-essays were noncontroversial, and did not advance Hannah-Jones's narrative about the American Revolution or Desmond's faulty economic claims.

To the extent that historians informed the project's discussion of the crucial period between 1775 and 1865, the *Times* has remained entirely nontransparent. Hannah-Jones has declined to specify which experts she consulted for her essay, and the only public acknowledgment of any outside review to date has come from Leslie Harris, the historian the *Times* recruited to fact-check her arguments about slavery's role in the American Revolution—and then promptly ignored when Harris advised against publishing the claim.[7] Desmond's essay sources its interpretation to seven academic historians who are quoted in the article. Yet all seven are affiliated with the "New History of Capitalism" (NHC) movement—an insular and ideological school of slavery scholars that emerged in the last decade, and that has fared poorly under scrutiny of its own arguments about slavery's economic dimensions.[8] Desmond's essay is, at best, a sloppy cribbing of NHC arguments that most other economists and non-NHC historians of slavery already found wanting and rejected.

Although the project's creator and defenders will likely continue to maintain that it is based on sound historical scholarship, this claim is at best only true for its less controversial treatments of the 20th century and more recent topics in race relations. Insofar as the history of slavery is concerned, though, the *New York Times* dropped the ball and delegated this content to either its own journalistic ranks or to nonspecialists like Desmond. The errors of fact and interpretation that ensued were entirely avoidable, and even to this day could be corrected if the *Times* would make a conscientious effort to engage with and respond to criticisms.

Instead, the newspaper has opted to stick by Hannah-Jones's political purposes at the expense of its historical accuracy—an editorial decision that unfortunately casts a shadow over the credibility of the entire project, when it might have easily been confined to only two or three of its essays.

Ironically, it is the *Times* itself that has given fodder to its political critics on the right. It did so through a year of dismissive derision against more responsible scrutiny from across the political spectrum, and by attempting to pass off an exercise in highly politicized editorial journalism as a substantive and classroom-ready contribution to the history and historiography of slavery—but only when it was convenient to invoke such claims. We need not indulge the bombastic posturing of Trump, or unlikely legislative efforts to strip funding from schools, to conclude that the 1619 Project is still ill-suited for K–12 education. That is a judgment we may make on its scholarly shortcomings alone.

12

Down the 1619 Project's Memory Hole

When Nikole Hannah-Jones launched the 1619 Project in August 2019, she emblazoned her Twitter profile with a New York Times–*produced graphic showing the year 1776 stricken out and replaced by the year 1619. The image aimed to highlight one of the most provocative claims in her original essay: that 1619, and not 1776, was the "true founding" of the United States, and with it a legacy of slavery that infused every aspect of the American project. The line immediately attracted controversy, and Hannah-Jones doubled down on the claim in her public appearances, commentaries, and Twitter feed.*

By spring 2020, the Covid-19 pandemic and accompanying lockdowns supplanted the academic debate over the 1619 Project's accuracy in the news cycle, save for brief bouts of attention such as the controversial decision to award Hannah-Jones a Pulitzer Prize in commentary for her lead essay. The 1619 Project debate returned with a fury in September 2020 as a part of the presidential election. Seeking to capitalize on the issue, President Donald Trump announced a "1776 Commission" and tasked it with producing a competing report to challenge the 1619 Project. Trump's foray into American history had the regrettable effect of reducing the heretofore scholarly debate into an election season sideshow, although Hannah-Jones shares in this culpability. A vocal supporter of Democratic candidate Joseph R. Biden, on September 18, 2020, she leaped into the political fray on a CNN broadcast to do battle with Trump's verbal jabs.

I recall watching this event in real time, though not for the political theater. Hannah-Jones opened her remarks by denying that she ever intended to displace 1776 with an alternative founding date. I was not the only person to notice this stunning reversal in Hannah-Jones's narrative. Baffled by this new line, Conor Friedersdorf of the Atlantic *and Robby Soave of* Reason Magazine *both posted examples of Hannah-Jones's previous media appearances in which she spoke of 1619 as the "true founding." I recalled the original line from the* New York Times*'s website and went to locate it for a quotation. To my shock, I found that the newspaper had changed the published text on its website and removed this claim in the intervening months. After a little sleuthing on archived copies of the newspaper's website, I ascertained that the edits occurred around January 2020, as Hannah-Jones's essay was being considered for the Pulitzer Prize. The newspaper had ghost-edited the most controversial line from the 1619 Project without any disclosure.*

I broke the story of these surreptitious edits in an essay for Quillette *magazine the following day. In doing so, I unintentionally ignited a firestorm in the* New York Times*'s newsroom. After my discovery, Hannah-Jones unleashed a barrage of denial on her Twitter feed. In a series of now-deleted tweets, she insisted that "there were no 'stealth corrections'" and that the text remained "unchanged" despite unambiguous evidence showing otherwise.* Times *columnist Bret Stephens took notice of Hannah-Jones's breach of journalistic ethics and devoted his weekly column to investigating the textual alterations.[1] As Stephens reported, Hannah-Jones remained adamant in her denials about the textual changes and offered excuses about her previous media appearances, claiming that the date comparison was only "metaphorical." On social media, she also portrayed herself as the victim of an unfair attack in which Stephens breached the solidarity of the newspaper by airing its dirty laundry in public.*

I have since described the events of September 2020 as the moment when the 1619 Project passed the point of no return into partisan political advocacy. Previous disputes concerned the factual accuracy of its content as Hannah-Jones attempted to straddle the line between historical scholarship and opinion advocacy. After the ghost-editing revelations, the textual integrity of the project itself became its most prominent defect. And despite clear evidence of these surreptitious edits, Hannah-Jones remained incorrigible about that fact.

THE HISTORY OF the American Revolution isn't the only thing the *New York Times* is revising through its 1619 Project. The "paper of record" has also taken to quietly altering the published text of the project itself after one of its claims came under intense criticism.

When the 1619 Project went to print in August 2019 as a special edition of the *New York Times Magazine*, the newspaper put up an interactive version on its website. The original opening text stated:

> The 1619 project is a major initiative from The New York Times observing the 400th anniversary of the beginning of American slavery. It aims to reframe the country's history, *understanding 1619 as our true founding,* and placing the consequences of slavery and the contributions of black Americans at the very center of our national narrative. (Emphasis added.)[2]

The passage, and in particular its description of the year 1619 as "our true founding," quickly became a flashpoint for controversy around the project. Critics on both the left and right took issue with the paper's declared intention of displacing 1776 with the alternative date—a point that was also emphasized in the magazine feature's graphics, showing the date of American independence crossed out and replaced by the date of the first slave ship's arrival in Jamestown, Virginia.

For several months after the 1619 Project first launched, its creator and organizer Nikole Hannah-Jones doubled down on the claim. "I argue that 1619 is our true founding," she tweeted the week after the project launched.[3] "Also, look at the banner pic in my profile"—a reference to the graphic of the date 1776 crossed out with a line. It's a claim she repeated many times over.[4]

But something changed as the historical controversies around the 1619 Project intensified in late 2019 and early 2020. A group of five distinguished historians took issue with Hannah-Jones's lead essay, focusing on its historically unsupported claim that protecting slavery was a primary motive of the American revolutionaries when they broke away from Britain in 1776. Other details of the project soon came under scrutiny, revealing both errors of fact

98 | *The 1619 Project Myth*

and dubious interpretations of evidence in other essays, such as Matthew Desmond's 1619 Project piece attempting to connect American capitalism with slavery.[5] Finally, back in March, a historian whom the *Times* recruited to fact-check Hannah-Jones's essay revealed that she had warned the paper against publishing its claims about the motives of the American Revolution on account of their weak evidence.[6] The 1619 Project's editors ignored the advice.

Throughout the controversy, the line about the year 1619 being "our true founding" continued to haunt the *Times*. This criticism did not aim to denigrate the project's titular date or the associated events in the history of slavery. Rather, the passage came to symbolize the *Times*'s blurring of historical analysis with editorial hyperbole. The announced intention of reframing the country's origin date struck many readers across the political spectrum as an implicit repudiation of the American revolution and its underlying principles.[7]

Rather than address this controversy directly, the *Times*, it now appears, decided to send it down the memory hole—the euphemized term for selectively editing inconvenient passages out of old newspaper reports in George Orwell's dystopian novel *1984*. Without announcement or correction, the newspaper quietly edited out the offending passage such that it now reads:

> The 1619 Project is an ongoing initiative from The New York Times Magazine that began in August 2019, the 400th anniversary of the beginning of American slavery. It aims to reframe the country's history by placing the consequences of slavery and the contributions of black Americans at the very center of our national narrative.

Discovery of this edit came about earlier that week when Nikole Hannah-Jones went on CNN to deny that she had ever sought to displace 1776 with a new founding date of 1619.[8] She repeated the point in a now-deleted tweet: "The #1619Project does not argue that 1619 was our true founding. We know this nation marks its founding at 1776."[9] It was not the first time that Hannah-Jones had tried to alter her self-depiction of the project's aims on account of the controversial line. She attempted a similar revision a few months ago during an online spat with conservative commentator Ben Shapiro.[10]

100 | *The 1619 Project Myth*

> In August of 1619, a ship appeared on this horizon, near Point Comfort, a coastal port in the British colony of Virginia. It carried more than 20 enslaved Africans, who were sold to the colonists. America was not yet America, but this was the moment it began. No aspect of the country that would be formed here has been untouched by the 250 years of slavery that followed. On the 400th anniversary of this fateful moment, it is finally time to tell our story truthfully.
>
> **The 1619 Project**

But this time the brazen rewriting of her own arguments proved too much. Hannah-Jones's readers scoured her own Twitter feed and public statements over the previous year, unearthing multiple instances where she had in fact announced an intention to displace 1776 with 1619.

The foremost piece of evidence against Hannah-Jones's spin, of course, came from the opening passage of the *Times*'s own website where it originally announced its aim "to reframe the country's history" around the year "1619 as our true founding." When readers returned to that website to cite the line, however, they discovered to their surprise that it was no longer there.

The *Times* quietly dropped the offending passage at some point during the intervening year, although multiple screencaps of the original exist. The Internet Archive's Wayback Machine suggests the alteration came around late December 2019, when the 1619 Project was facing an onslaught of criticism over this exact point from several distinguished historians of the American founding.

It wasn't the only edit that the newspaper made to further conceal its previous denigration of 1776. Prompted by the discovery of the first deletion, Twitter users noticed another suspicious change to the project's text.[11] The print edition of the 1619 Project from August 2019 contained an introductory passage reading:

> In August of 1619, a ship appeared on this horizon, near Point Comfort, a coastal port in the British colony of Virginia. It carried more than 20 enslaved Africans, who were sold to the colonists. America was not yet America, but this was the moment it began. No aspect of the country that would be formed here has been untouched by the 250 years of slavery that followed.[12]

Down the 1619 Project's Memory Hole | 101

> In August of 1619, a ship appeared on this horizon, near Point Comfort, a coastal port in the English colony of Virginia. It carried more than 20 enslaved Africans, who were sold to the colonists. No aspect of the country that would be formed here has been untouched by the years of slavery that followed. On the 400th anniversary of this fateful moment, it is finally time to tell our story truthfully.

The website version of the 1619 Project now reads:

> In August of 1619, a ship appeared on this horizon, near Point Comfort, a coastal port in the English colony of Virginia. It carried more than 20 enslaved Africans, who were sold to the colonists. No aspect of the country that would be formed here has been untouched by the years of slavery that followed.[13]

The additional reference to the 1619 origin point, found in the original print version, is no more.

Whatever the exact occasion for the changes, the *Times* did not disclose its edits or how they obscured one of the most controversial claims in the entire 1619 Project. It simply made the problematic passages disappear, hoping that nobody would notice.

13

The Suicide of the American Historical Association

The initial scholarly debate about the 1619 Project brought together an unusual and cross-political coalition of responses. I entered this discussion as an economic historian who studies slavery, but also as a classical liberal who works on the historical connections between free market economic thinkers and the abolitionist movement. I soon found myself in unexpected company as the World Socialist Web Site *(WSWS) published a series of interviews with several left-of-center academic historians offering similar criticisms of the 1619 Project's claims. The left-of-center critics included several highly regarded historians, such as Sean Wilentz, James Oakes, and James M. McPherson. Almost all came from the senior ranks of academia. They were holders of endowed chairs or distinguished emeritus faculty. By contrast, many younger historians on the left either decided to sit the debate out or offered generic endorsements of the 1619 Project's objectives without specifically addressing its controversial claims.*

The reason for this generational gap among the 1619 Project's critics and proponents on the left became more apparent as Nikole Hannah-Jones leaned into overt political advocacy, particularly after the 2020 election. Most of the project's left-leaning detractors enjoyed the benefit of career security, tenure, or even retirement from teaching. At the same time most of its scholarly critics from non-left perspectives enjoyed job security outside of the American university system. Scholars who lacked either of these two conditions risked negative career repercussions for speaking out about the substandard historical arguments contained in the New York Times's *narrative.*

1619 Project founder Nikole Hannah-Jones often led the attacks on her critics with a barrage of name-calling and similar unprofessional antics on her Twitter feed. She denounced the WSWS authors as "white historians" and dismissed their academic qualifications with little more than sneering derision. I faced similar scorn from Hannah-Jones's keyboard, usually consisting of attacks on my qualifications. "What are the credentials, exactly of Phil Magness?" she tweeted in January 2020. Over the next four years, similar insinuations would become a recurring theme of Hannah-Jones's retorts to me—and to almost every other scholar who critically examined her claims. She did not need to answer the 1619 Project's critics because, in her mind, we lacked the expertise even to evaluate her work.

Hannah-Jones's penchant for unscholarly vilification had a chilling effect upon subsequent commentary, particularly among writers who recognized the historical deficiencies in the 1619 Project's analysis but lacked the job security or thickness of skin to endure the ensuing barrage of insults. This ugly pattern reached its pinnacle in the summer of 2022 when James H. Sweet, then-president of the American Historical Association, published a commentary article decrying the politicization of the history profession by activists on both the left and the right. Sweet's indictment of political "presentism" began with the misuse of historical evidence by right-leaning sources to promote partisan narratives about constitutional history, but he also cited the 1619 Project's own political turn as an example of the same tendencies on the left. Hannah-Jones responded by unleashing a stream of social media scorn and a Twitter mob to follow it. Within hours of Sweet's column going live, he faced a full-fledged "cancellation" campaign for the sin of criticizing the 1619 Project.

I wrote the following article as this shameful episode unfolded in real time. Notably, none of Sweet's detractors ever meaningfully challenged his mild criticisms of Hannah-Jones on factual grounds. Simply saying anything negative about the 1619 Project at all made him "guilty," as doing so broke the ranks of solidarity with the project's increasingly pronounced political objectives. Within a day of these events, Sweet capitulated to the Twitter mob by issuing an apol-

*ogy statement for the "harm" he committed by writing his column.[1]
The apology offered no specific details on the nature of this alleged
"harm," let alone an explanation of why it required a public confession. To observers, the intended message was clear: the very act of
criticizing Hannah-Jones's work constituted a grievous moral offense
among the academic left, and even senior members of the profession
could be demonized for defying the 1619 Project's political narrative.*

A BIZARRE STRING of events is unfolding at the American
Historical Association (AHA). In the August 2022 issue of the organization's
magazine, AHA president James H. Sweet published a column about the
problem of "presentism" in academic historical writing. According to Sweet,
an unsettling number of academic historians have allowed their political views
in the present to shape and distort their interpretations of the past.

Sweet offered a gentle criticism of the *New York Times*'s 1619 Project as
evidence of this pattern. Many historians embraced the 1619 Project for its
political messages despite substantive flaws of fact and interpretation in its
content. Sweet thus asked: "As journalism, the project is powerful and effective, but is it history?"[2]

Within moments of his column appearing online, all hell broke loose on
Twitter.

Incensed at even the mildest suggestion that politicization was undermining the integrity of historical scholarship, the activist wing of the history
profession showed up on the AHA's thread and began demanding Sweet's
cancellation. Cate Denial, a professor of history at Knox College, led the
charge with a widely retweeted thread calling on colleagues to bombard the
AHA's Executive Board with emails protesting Sweet's column.[3] "We cannot
let this fizzle," she declared before posting a list of about 20 email addresses.

Other activist historians joined in, flooding the thread with profanity-
laced attacks on Sweet's race and gender as well as calls for his resignation over
a disliked opinion column. The responses were almost universally devoid of
any substance.[4] None challenged Sweet's argument in any meaningful way.
It was sufficient enough for him to have harbored the "wrong" thoughts—to
have questioned the scholarly rigor of activism-infused historical writing, and
to have criticized the 1619 Project in even the mildest terms.

Ida Bae Wells ✓
@nhannahjones

I've always said that the 1619 Project is not a history. It is a work of journalism that explicitly seeks to challenge the national narrative and, therefore, the national memory. The project has always been as much about the present as it is the past.

9:29 AM · Jul 27, 2020 · Twitter for iPhone

New York Times columnist and 1619 Project contributor Jamelle Bouie jumped in, casually dismissing Sweet's concerns over the politicization of scholarship with contemporary "social justice" issues.[5] 1619 Project creator Nikole Hannah-Jones retweeted the attacks on Sweet, even though she has previously invoked the "journalistic" and editorial nature of her project to shield it from scholarly criticism by historians.

Other activist historians such as the New School's Claire Potter retorted that the 1619 Project was indeed scholarly history, insisting that "big chunks of it are written by professional, award-winning historians."[6] Sweet was therefore in the wrong to call it journalism, or to question its scholarly accuracy.

Potter's claims are deeply misleading.[7] Only 2 of the 1619 Project's 12 feature essays were written by historians, and neither of them are specialists in the crucial period between 1776 and 1865, when slavery was at its peak. The controversial parts of the 1619 Project were all written by opinion journalists such as Hannah-Jones, or nonexperts writing well outside of their own competencies such as Matthew Desmond.[8]

The frenzy further exposed the very same problems in the profession that Sweet's essay cautioned against. David Austin Walsh, a historian at the University of Virginia, took issue with historians offering *any* public criticism of the 1619 Project's flaws—no matter their validity—because those criticisms are "going to be weaponized by the right."[9] In Walsh's hyperpoliticized worldview,[10] historical accuracy is wholly subordinate to the political objectives of the project. Sweet's sin in telling the truth about the 1619 Project's defects was being "willfully blind to the predictable political consequences of [his] public interventions." Any argument that does not advance a narrow band of far-left political activism is not only unfit for sharing—it must be suppressed.

Message from James H. Sweet

My September *Perspectives on History* column has generated anger and dismay among many of our colleagues and members. I take full responsibility that it did not convey what I intended and for the harm that it has caused. I had hoped to open a conversation on how we "do" history in our current politically charged environment. Instead, I foreclosed this conversation for many members, causing harm to colleagues, the discipline, and the Association.

A president's monthly column, one of the privileges of the elected office, provides a megaphone to the membership and the discipline. The views and opinions expressed in that column are not those of the Association. If my ham-fisted attempt at provocation has proven anything, it is that the AHA membership is as vocal and robust as ever. If anyone has criticisms that they have been reluctant or unable to post publicly, please feel free to contact me directly.

I sincerely regret the way I have alienated some of my Black colleagues and friends. I am deeply sorry. In my clumsy efforts to draw attention to methodological flaws in teleological presentism, I left the impression that questions posed from absence, grief, memory, and resilience somehow matter less than those posed from positions of power. This absolutely is not true. It wasn't my intention to leave that impression, but my provocation completely missed the mark.

Once again, I apologize for the damage I have caused to my fellow historians, the discipline, and the AHA. I hope to redeem myself in future conversations with you all. I'm listening and learning.

Within hours of the AHA's original tweet of Sweet's article, the cancellation campaign was in full swing. Predictably, the AHA caved to the cancellers.

One day after the offending article went live, the AHA tweeted out a public apology from Sweet.[11] It reads like a forced confession statement, acknowledging the "harm" and "damage" allegedly caused by simply raising questions about the politicization of scholarship toward overtly ideological activist ends. It did not matter that Sweet's criticisms were mild and couched in plenty of nuance, or that they even came from a center-left perspective that also criticized conservative historians for politicizing the debate around gun rights. Sweet was guilty of pointing out that partisan political activism undermines scholarly rigor when the lines between the two blur, because the overwhelming majority of that activism inside the history profession currently comes from the political left. And for that, the very same activists extracted an obsequious apology letter. Its text, reproduced above, reads like a "struggle session" for academic wrongthink.

Sweet's apology excited the activist wing of the profession, though it did little to placate their ire.[12] The resignation demands continued, because Sweet's apology was "insincere" and because his argument would be used by the "wrong" people—i.e., anyone who dissents from a particular brand of

108 | *The 1619 Project Myth*

progressive activist orthodoxy.[13] Simply criticizing the 1619 Project would play into the tactics of "Right-wingers, Nazis, and other bad-faith actors" who could use Sweet's commentary "in the service of white supremacism and misogyny," announced Kevin Gannon, a historian who's primarily known for scolding other scholars on Twitter when they deviate from the profession's far-left orthodoxies.[14]

In this branch of academia, it does not matter whether the 1619 Project was truthful or factually accurate. The only concerns are whether its narrative can be weaponized for a political cause or used to deflect scrutiny of the same. As is often the case in the pseudo-moralizing political crusades of academia, the loudest demands against Sweet also came from the least productive academics—historians with thin CVs and little in the way of original scholarly research to their names, although they do maintain 24-7 Twitter feeds of progressive political commentary.

Lora Burnett, one of the more vocal cancellation crusaders after the initial article posted, scoffed at Sweet, announcing that "this apology was basically, 'sorry I made you sad but I'm still right.'"[15] She continued: "Lamenting 'inartful expression' is apparently easier than admitting to flawed argument, unsupported claims, and factually incorrect assertions."[16] Note that Burnett and the other detractors never bothered to explain how Sweet's argument was flawed or unsupported. Nor did they attempt to pen a rebuttal, which could have produced a constructive dialogue about the role of political activism in shaping historical scholarship. It was sufficient to denounce him as guilty for holding the wrong opinions. No matter the apology that Sweet made, the campaign to eject him from the history profession's markedly impolite company would continue.

Meanwhile, the rest of the world began to take notice of the bizarre spectacle playing out at the main professional organization for a major academic discipline. As criticisms mounted on the AHA's Twitter feed, the organization moved to shut down debate entirely. It locked its Twitter account, and posted a message to members denouncing the public blowback as the product of "trolls" and "bad faith actors."

Keep in mind that only 24 hours earlier, the AHA had no problem with hundreds of activist historians flooding its threads with actual harassing behavior by bad faith actors. It tolerated cancellation threats directed against

its president, calls to flood the personal email accounts of its board with harassing messages and denunciations of Sweet, and dozens of profane, sexist, and personally degrading attacks on Sweet himself. There were no AHA denunciations of those "trolls" or their "appalling" behavior, and no statements calling for "civil discourse" while the activist Twitterstorian mobs flooded the original thread with obscenity-laced vitriol and ad hominem attacks on Sweet.

Sadly, this type of unprofessional belligerence is now the norm on History Twitter.[17] It would never be tolerated from any other perspective than the far left, but it is valorized in the profession as long as it serves that particular set of ideological objectives.

The final irony is that the AHA only shuttered its Twitter feed from the public when it could no longer restrict the conversation to the activist mob calling for Sweet's cancellation. It's the same brand of intellectual closure that Sweet's offending column warned against in its final passage: "When we foreshorten or shape history to justify rather than inform contemporary political positions, we not only undermine the discipline but threaten its very integrity."

14

The 1619 Project Unrepentantly Pushes Junk History

The scholarly controversies surrounding the 1619 Project exposed a major shortcoming of the original project, as published in the New York Times Magazine. *The newspaper launched this flagship venture without properly vetting its most controversial claims with fact-checkers. In the most notorious instance, the* Times *ignored the counsel of its own fact-checker Leslie M. Harris, a historian of early America who tried to warn Hannah-Jones that the evidence did not support the 1619 Project's reinvention of the American Revolution as a contest between pro-slavery colonies and anti-slavery Great Britain. The 1619 Project appears not to have even used basic fact-checking on Matthew Desmond's article about the economics of slavery and, further, brushed aside good-faith efforts to correct its many factual and interpretive errors. In both instances, the chapters facing the most scrutiny were written by nonexperts with tenuous grasps of the complex historiographical debates surrounding their topics and even less familiarity with the existing scholarly literature. Hannah-Jones's interpretation of the American Revolution appears to have originated as a garbled rendering of Lerone Bennett Jr.'s 1962 book* Before the Mayflower: A History of the Negro in America 1619–1962, *albeit stripped of Bennett's efforts to engage the existing literature. Desmond provided an amateur synopsis of the post-2010 New History of Capitalism school's main texts, repeating these authors' most ideological claims at face value and offering no awareness of the deeper scholarly literature on slavery's economics that preceded this body of work.*

When Hannah-Jones set out to expand the 1619 Project into a 600-page hardcover edition, her unspoken but readily apparent aim included an attempt to retrofit scholarly heft into the unelaborated historical claims of the original publication. The resulting book contained expanded versions of the problematic chapters by Hannah-Jones and Desmond, each ostensibly answering their critics by backfilling their narratives with footnotes to academic works. Hannah-Jones padded her essay with citations to revisionist accounts of the American Revolution by historians including Woody Holton, David Waldstreicher, and Gerald Horne. Her original essay evinced no awareness of these works, and her expanded account made no effort to situate their heterodox claims within the broader scholarly literature on slavery in the American Revolution. Instead, she simply cherry-picked a handful of passages from secondary works that narrowly aligned with her prior arguments and appended them as footnotes to her already-formulated positions. Desmond quietly modified two of the most egregious factual errors in his original piece, after steadfastly refusing corrections to the newspaper edition. He retained his overall political argument in unmodified form, however, and overlaid it with an eccentric and ideologically loaded application of Marxist class theory to the postbellum U.S. economy.

Hannah-Jones also recruited new authors to join the project; Ibram X. Kendi authored a new chapter, and Hannah-Jones included new citations to Kendi's work in her own essay. One of the only substantive modifications to Hannah-Jones's original argument pertained to her assessment of Abraham Lincoln's colonization program. As I documented in the first edition of this book, many of Hannah-Jones's early critics missed the mark by dismissing her discussion of Lincoln. I have the unusual distinction of having defended her on this narrow point, even as I criticized the larger project. But Hannah-Jones also made use of my own original scholarship to defend the 1619 Project at the time of its original August 2019 release. She specifically cited my 2011 book Colonization After Emancipation: Lincoln and the Movement for Black Resettlement *as evidence that other historians had erred in prematurely dismissing*

Lincoln's connection to black colonization efforts during the Civil War. In another now-deleted comment, she even linked to a 2013 article about Lincoln and colonization that I wrote for the New York Times, *albeit without realizing that I was the author.*[1] *Shortly thereafter Hannah-Jones recognized me as a critic of the 1619 Project. Almost instantly, a characteristic barrage of personal vilification appeared on Hannah-Jones's Twitter feed. I had been demoted from a repeatedly cited authority on the colonization movement to persona non grata in her mind.*

In the 2022 book edition, Hannah-Jones further indulged this petty spite by excising my scholarship entirely and abandoning her previous depictions of Lincoln. In its place appeared a new footnote to Kendi, whose 2016 book Stamped from the Beginning *repeats an older and factually erroneous secondary literature that attempts to distance Lincoln from the colonization program. As with the revisionist literature on the revolution, Hannah-Jones structured her search for footnotes based on whether she could weaponize them in service of her own political narratives about the American past—and, in this case, her own personal battles with a critic.*

I composed the following essay as a feature article on the 1619 Project book for Reason Magazine. *It summarizes the main differences between the original essays by Hannah-Jones and Desmond and their expanded versions in the hardcover edition. Although Hannah-Jones has since portrayed the book as a "peer-reviewed" addendum that allegedly responded to her critics and tightened her arguments, its text tells a different story. Hannah-Jones and Desmond overlaid the flaws in their original essays with additional errors of fact and interpretation. The result was a book-length expansion of the 1619 Project that is substantially weaker, and substantially more ideological, than the original version from the print newspaper that it aimed to replace.*

"I TOO YEARN for universal justice," wrote Zora Neale Hurston in her autobiography, *Dust Tracks on a Road*, "but how to bring it about is another thing." The black novelist's remarks prefaced a passage where she grappled with the historical legacy of slavery in the African-American experience. Perhaps unexpectedly, Hurston informed her readers that she had "no intention of wasting my time beating on old graves with a club."[2]

Hurston did not aim to bury an ugly past but to search for historical understanding. Her 1927 interview with Cudjoe Lewis, among the last living survivors of the 1860 voyage of the slave ship *Clotilda,* contains an invaluable eyewitness account of the middle passage as told by one of its victims. Yet Hurston saw only absurdity in trying to find justice by bludgeoning the past for its sins. "While I have a handkerchief over my eyes crying over the landing of the first slaves in 1619," she continued, "I might miss something swell that is going on in" the present day.[3]

Hurston's writings present an intriguing foil to the *New York Times*'s 1619 Project, which the newspaper recently expanded into a book-length volume. As its subtitle announces, the book aims to cultivate a "new origin story" of the United States where the turmoil and strife of the past are infused into a living present as tools for attaining a particular vision of justice. Indeed, it restores the 1619 Project's original aim of displacing the "mythology" of 1776 "to reframe the country's history, understanding 1619 as our true founding." This passage was quietly deleted from the *New York Times*'s website in early 2020 just as the embattled journalistic venture was making a bid for a Pulitzer Prize. After a brief foray into self-revisionism in which she denied ever making such a claim, editor Nikole Hannah-Jones has now apparently brought this objective back to the forefront of the 1619 Project.

Vacillating claims about the 1619 Project's purpose have come to typify Hannah-Jones's argumentation. In similar fashion, she selectively describes the project as a work either of journalism or of scholarly history, as needed. Yet as the stealth editing of the "true founding" passage revealed, these pivots are often haphazardly executed. So too is her attempt to claim the mantle of Hurston. In a recent public spat with Andrew Sullivan, Hannah-Jones accused the British political commentator of "ignorance" for suggesting that "Zora Neale Hurston's work sits in opposition to mine." She was apparently unaware that *Dust Tracks on a Road* anticipated and rejected the premise of the 1619 Project eight decades prior to its publication.

On the surface, *The 1619 Project: A New Origin Story* (One World) expands the short essays from the *New York Times* print edition into almost 600 pages of text, augmented by additional chapters and authors. The unmistakable subtext is an opportunity to answer the barrage of controversies that surrounded the project after its publication in August 2019. "We wanted to learn from the discussions that surfaced after the project's publication and address the criticisms some historians offered in good faith," Hannah-Jones announces in the book's introduction, before devoting the majority of her ink to denouncing the blusterous critical pronouncements of the Trump administration after it targeted the 1619 Project in the run-up to the 2020 presidential election. Serious scholarly interlocutors of the original project are largely sidestepped, and factual errors in the original text are either glossed over or quietly removed.

While the majority of the public discussion around the 1619 Project has focused on Hannah-Jones's lead essay, its greatest defects appear in the Princeton sociologist Matthew Desmond's essay "Capitalism." Hannah-Jones's writings provide the framing for the project, but Desmond supplies its ideological core—a political charge to radically reorient the basic structure of the American economy so as to root out an alleged slavery-infused brutality from capitalism.

Hannah-Jones's prescriptive call for slavery reparations flows seamlessly from Desmond's argument, as does her own expanded historical narrative—most recently displayed in a lecture series for MasterClass in which she attempted to explain the causes of the 2008 financial crisis by faulting slavery. "The tendrils of [slavery] can still be seen in modern capitalism," she declared, where banking companies "were repackaging risky bonds and risky notes . . . in ways [that] none of us really understood." The causal mechanism connecting the two events remained imprecise, save for allusions to "risky slave bonds" and a redesignation of the cotton industry as "too big to fail."

Making what appears to be a muddled reference to the Panic of 1837, she confidently declared that "what happened in 1830 is what happened in 2008." The claimed connection aimed to prove that the "American capitalist system is defined today by the long legacy and shadow of slavery." This racist, brutal system "offers the least protections for workers of all races," she said, and it thus warrants a sweeping overhaul through the political instruments of the state. To this end, Hannah-Jones appends an expanded essay to *The 1619 Project* book, endorsing a Duke University study's call for a "vast social transformation produced by the adoption of bold national policies."

"At the center of those policies," she declared, "must be reparations."

Uncorrected Errors

What are we to make of the 1619 Project's anti-capitalism in light of the new book's expanded treatment? For context, let's consider how Desmond handles the defects of his original argument.

In his quest to tie modern capitalism to slavery, Desmond began with a genealogical claim. Antebellum plantation owners employed double-entry accounting and record-keeping practices, some of them quite sophisticated. A more careful historian might note that such practices date back to the Italian banking families of the late Middle Ages, or point out that accounting is far from a distinctively capitalist institution. After all, even the central planners of the Soviet Union attempted to meticulously track raw material inputs, labor capacity, and multi-year productivity goals. Does this make the gulags a secret bastion of free market capitalism? Though seemingly absurd, such conclusions are the logical extension of Desmond's argument. "When an accountant depreciates an asset to save on taxes or when a midlevel manager spends an afternoon filling in rows and columns on an Excel spreadsheet," he wrote in the original newspaper edition, "they are repeating business procedures whose roots twist back to slave-labor camps."

Setting aside this unusual leap of logic, the claim rests upon a basic factual error. Desmond attributed this genealogy to the UC Berkeley historian Caitlin Rosenthal's 2018 book on plantation financial record keeping, *Accounting for Slavery*. Yet Rosenthal warned against using her work as an "origin story" for modern capitalism. She "did not find a simple path," she wrote, by which plantation accounting books "evolved into Microsoft Excel." Desmond, it appears, made a basic reading error.

When I first pointed out this mistake to Jake Silverstein, the editor in chief of the *New York Times Magazine*, in early 2020, he demurred on making any correction. After consulting with Rosenthal, the *Times* passed off this inversion of phrasing as an interpretive difference between the two authors. In the new book version of Desmond's essay, the troublesome Microsoft Excel line disappears without any explanation, although Desmond retains anachronistic references to the plantation owners' "spreadsheets." As with other controversies from the 1619 Project, the revisions pair a cover-up of an error with haphazard execution.

The 1619 Project Unrepentantly Pushes Junk History | 117

This pattern persists and compounds through the meatier parts of Desmond's expanded thesis. His original essay singles out American capitalism as "peculiarly brutal"—an economy characterized by aggressive price competition, consumerism, diminished labor union power, and soaring inequality. This familiar list of progressive grievances draws on its own array of suspect sources. For example, Desmond leans heavily on the empirical work of the UC Berkeley economists Emmanuel Saez and Gabriel Zucman to depict a society plagued by the growing concentration of wealth among the "top 1 percent." Data from the Federal Reserve suggest that these two authors exaggerate the rise in wealth concentration since 1990 by almost double the actual number.[4] Desmond's own twist is to causally link this present-day talking point with the economic legacy of slavery.

To do so, he draws upon recent statistical analysis that showed a 400 percent expansion in cotton production from 1800 to 1860. In Desmond's telling, this growth stems from the capitalistic refinement of violence to extract labor out of human chattel. "Plantation owners used a combination of incentives and punishments to squeeze as much as possible out of enslaved workers," he declared—a carefully calibrated and systematized enterprise of torture to maximize production levels. In the original essay, Desmond sourced this thesis to Cornell historian Edward E. Baptist, whose book *The Half Has Never Been Told* essentially revived the old "King Cotton" thesis of American economic development that the Confederacy embraced on the eve of the Civil War. Baptist's book is a foundational text of the "New History of Capitalism" (NHC) school of historiography. The 1619 Project, in turn, leans almost exclusively on NHC scholars for its economic interpretations.

But Baptist's thesis fared poorly after its publication in 2014, mainly because he misrepresented the source of his cotton growth statistics. The numbers come from a study by the economists Alan L. Olmstead of the University of California, Davis, and Paul W. Rhode, then with the University of Arizona, who empirically demonstrated the 400 percent production increase before the Civil War but then linked it to a very different cause.[5] Cotton output did not grow because of refinements in the calibrated torture of slaves, but rather as a result of improved seed technology that increased the plant's yield. In 2018, Olmstead and Rhode published a damning dissection of the NHC literature that both disproved the torture thesis and documented what

118 | *The 1619 Project Myth*

appear to be intentional misrepresentations of evidence by Baptist, including his treatment of their own numbers.[6] Olmstead and Rhode in no way dispute the horrific brutality of slavery. They simply show that beatings were not the causal mechanism driving cotton's economic expansion, as the NHC literature claims.

As with Desmond's other errors, I brought these problems to the attention of Silverstein with a request for a factual correction in late 2019. Almost two years later I finally received an answer: Desmond replied that "Baptist made a causal claim linking violence to productivity on cotton plantations," whereas his "article did not make such a casual [*sic*] claim." I leave the reader to judge the accuracy of this statement against the 1619 Project's original text, including its explicit attribution of the argument to Baptist.

Even more peculiar is how Desmond handled the "calibrated torture" thesis in the book edition. In the paragraph where he previously named Baptist as his source, he now writes that "Alan Olmstead and Paul Rhode found that improved cotton varieties enabled hands to pick more cotton per day." But this is far from a correction. Desmond immediately appends this sentence with an unsubstantiated caveat: "But advanced techniques that improved upon ways to manage land and labor surely played their part as well." In excising Baptist's name, he simply reinserts Baptist's erroneous claim without attribution, proceeding as if it has not meaningfully altered his argument.

In these and other examples, we find the defining characteristics of the 1619 Project's approach to history. Desmond and Hannah-Jones initiate their inquiries by adopting a narrow and heavily ideological narrative about our nation's past. They then enlist evidence as a weapon to support that narrative, or its modern-day political objectives. When that evidence falters under scrutiny, the 1619 Project's narrative does not change or adapt to account for a different set of facts. Instead, its authors simply swap out the discredited claim for another and proceed as if nothing has changed—as if no correction is necessary.

Ignoring the Fact-Checkers

We see the same pattern in how Hannah-Jones handles the most controversial claim in the original 1619 Project. Her opening essay there declared that "one of the primary reasons the colonists decided to declare their independence from Britain was because they wanted to protect the institution of slavery." In early 2020, Silverstein begrudgingly amended the passage online to read "*some of* the colonists" (emphasis added) after Northwestern University historian Leslie M. Harris revealed that, as one of the newspaper's fact-checkers, she had cautioned Hannah-Jones against making this claim, only to be ignored.

The ensuing litigation of this passage across editorial pages and Twitter threads unintentionally revealed an unsettling defect of the *Times*'s venture. The 1619 Project was not a heterodox challenge to conventional accounts of American history, as its promotional material insinuated. An endeavor of this sort could be commendable, if executed in a scholarly fashion. Instead, the original essays by Hannah-Jones and Desmond betray a deep and pervasive unfamiliarity with their respective subject matters.

When subject matter experts pointed out that Hannah-Jones exaggerated her arguments about the Revolution, or that Britain was not, in fact, an existential threat to American slavery in 1776 as she strongly suggested (the British Empire would take another 58 years before it emancipated its West Indian colonies), she unleashed a barrage of personally abusive derision toward the critics. Brown University's Gordon S. Wood and other Revolutionary War experts were dismissed as "white historians" for questioning her claims. When Princeton's James M. McPherson, widely considered the dean of living Civil War historians, chimed in, Hannah-Jones lashed out on Twitter: "Who considers him preeminent? I don't."

The 1619 Project did not simply disagree with these subject matter experts. Its editors and writers had failed to conduct a basic literature review of the scholarship around their contentions and subsequently stumbled their way into unsupported historical arguments. While some academic historians contributed essays on other subjects, none of the 1619 Project's feature articles on the crucial period from 1776 to 1865 came from experts in American slavery. Journalists such as Hannah-Jones took the lead, while highly specialized topics such as the economics of slavery were assigned to nonexperts like Desmond, whose scholarly résumé contained no prior engagement with that subject.

The book's revised introduction is less a corrective to the defects of the original than a mad scramble to retroactively paint a scholarly veneer over its weakest claims. Hannah-Jones leans heavily on secondary sources to backfill her own narrative with academic footnotes, but the product is more an exercise in cherry-picking than a historiographical analysis.

Consider the book's treatment of *Somerset v. Stewart*, the landmark 1772 British legal case that freed an enslaved captive aboard a ship in the London docks. Hannah-Jones appeals to the University of Virginia historian Alan Taylor, who wrote that "colonial masters felt shocked by the implication" of the case for the future of slavery in North America. Yet Taylor's elaboration focused narrowly on the case's negative reception in Virginia, while Hannah-Jones generalizes that into a claim that "the colonists took the ruling as an insult, as signaling that they were of inferior status" and threatening their slave property. Curiously missing from her discussion is the not insignificant reaction of Benjamin Franklin, who complained to his abolitionist friend Anthony Benezet that *Somerset* had not gone far enough. Britain, he wrote, had indulged a hypocrisy, and "piqued itself on its virtue, love of liberty, and the equity of its courts, in setting free a single negro" while maintaining a "detestable commerce by laws for promoting the Guinea trade" in slaves.[7]

To sustain her contention that a defense of slavery weighed heavily on the revolutionary cause, Hannah-Jones now latches her essay to the University of South Carolina historian Woody Holton—a familiar secondary source from graduate school seminars who appears to have crossed her path only after the initial controversy. Since its publication, Holton has united his efforts with the 1619 Project, focusing in particular on Lord Dunmore's proclamation of 1775 to argue that the document's promise of emancipation to the slaves of rebellious colonists had a galvanizing effect on the American cause.

Dunmore's decree—which offered freedom to slaves who fought for the crown—came about as a move of desperation to salvage his already-faltering control over the colony of Virginia. Holton and Hannah-Jones alike exaggerate its purpose beyond recognition. Holton has taken to calling it "Dunmore's Emancipation Proclamation," hoping to evoke President Abraham Lincoln's more famous document, and *The 1619 Project* book repeats the analogy. But all sense of proportion is lost in the comparison. Lincoln's measure, though military in nature, reflected his own long-standing anti-slavery beliefs. It freed 50,000 people almost immediately, and extended its reach to millions as the war progressed. Dunmore, by contrast, was a slaveowner with a particularly brutal reputation of his own. His decree likely freed no more than 2,000 slaves, primarily out of the hope that it would trigger a broader slave revolt, weaken the rebellion, and allow him to reassert British rule with the plantation system intact. Hannah-Jones also haphazardly pushes her evidence beyond even Holton's misleading claims. "For men like [George] Washington," she writes, "the Dunmore proclamation ignited the turn to independence." This is a curious anachronism, given that Washington assumed command of the Continental Army on June 15, 1775—some five months before Dunmore's order of November 7, 1775.

Fringe Scholars and Ideological Cranks

The same self-defeating pairing of aggressive historical claims and slipshod historical methodology extends into Desmond's expanded essay. Moving its modern-day political aims to the forefront, Desmond peddles a novel theory about the history of the Internal Revenue Service. "Progressive taxation remains among the best ways to limit economic inequality" and to fund an expansive welfare state, he asserts. Yet in Desmond's rendering, again invoking debunked statistical claims from Saez and Zucman, "America's present-day tax system . . . is regressive and insipid." The reason? He contends that the IRS is still hobbled by slavery—a historical legacy that allegedly deprives the tax collection agency of "adequate financial backing and administrative support."

It is true that slavery forced several compromises during the Constitutional Convention, including measures that constrained the allocation of the federal tax burden across the states. Yet Desmond's rendering of this history borders on incompetence. He declares that the Constitution's original privileging of import tariffs "stunted the bureaucratic infrastructure of the nation"—apparently oblivious to the fact that Alexander Hamilton's Treasury Department set up one of the first true national bureaucracies through the federal customs house system. To Desmond, the United States was a relative latecomer to income taxation because of a reactionary constitutional design that impeded democratic pressures for redistribution in the late 19th century. This too is in error. In fact, comparative analyses of historical tax adoption strongly suggest that less democratic countries with lower levels of enfranchisement were the first movers in the international shift toward income

122 | *The 1619 Project Myth*

taxation.[8] When the U.S. Congress passed the 16th Amendment in 1909 to establish a federal income tax, the first wave of ratifications came from the states of the old Confederacy, which saw it as a means of transferring the federal tax burden onto the Northeast.

At this point, Desmond's narrative veers from the fringes of academic discourse into ideological crankery. After a misplaced causal attribution of 19th-century development to the economic prowess of King Cotton, he turns his attention to what he sees as the true fault of American slavery: It allegedly enabled "capitalists" to leverage race "to divide workers—free from unfree, white from Black—diluting their collective power." This fracture among an otherwise natural class-based alliance is said to have impeded the emergence of a strong and explicitly socialistic labor movement in the United States, leading to "conditions for worker exploitation and inequality that exist to this day."

Desmond's theory makes sense only if one accepts the historical methodology of hardcore Marxist doctrine. History is supposed to progress toward the ascendance of the laboring class; thus, any failure of the proletarian revolution to materialize must arise from some ruling-class imposition. To Desmond, that imposition is slavery: "What should have followed [industrialization], Karl Marx and a long list of other political theorists predicted, was a large-scale labor movement. Factory workers made to log long hours under harsh conditions should have locked arms and risen up against their bosses, gaining political power in the formation of a Labor Party or even ushering in a socialist revolution."

After waxing about the "democratic socialism" of European welfare states, Desmond thus laments that "socialism never flourished here, and a defining feature of American capitalism is the country's relatively low level of labor power." This he considers slavery's legacy for the present day.

This thesis is bizarre, not to mention historically tone-deaf. The 19th-century abolitionist rallying cry of "free soil, free labor, free men" reflected an intellectual alliance between free market theory and emancipation. Nowhere was this more succinctly captured than in the words of pro-slavery theorist George Fitzhugh, who declared in 1854 that the doctrine of laissez-faire was "at war with all kinds of slavery."

Desmond's historical narrative is not original to the 1619 Project. It revives a line of argument first made in 1906 by the then-Marxist (and later National

Socialist) philosopher Werner Sombart. Asking why socialism never took hold in the United States, Sombart offered an answer: "the Negro question has directly removed any class character from each of the two [American political] parties," causing power to allocate on geographic rather than economic lines.[9] Desmond both credits and expands upon Sombart's thesis, writing: "As Northern elites were forging an industrial proletariat of factory workers . . . Southern elites . . . began creating an agrarian proletariat." Slavery's greatest economic fault, in this rendering, was not its horrific violation of individual liberty and dignity but its alleged intrusion upon a unified laboring class consciousness.

The great tragedy of the original 1619 Project was its missed opportunity to add detail, nuance, and reflection to our historical understanding of slavery and its legacy. That opportunity was lost not upon publication but in the aftermath, when the *New York Times* met its scholarly critics with insult and derision. The ensuing controversies, initially confined to Hannah-Jones's and Desmond's essays, came to overshadow the remainder of the project, including its other historical contributions as well as its literary and artistic sections.

The book version continues down this path, obscuring existing errors through textual sleights of hand and compounding them with fringe scholarship. The unifying theme of it all is not historical discovery or retrospection, but the pursuit of political power: less a historical reimagining of slavery's legacy than an activist manual for taxation and redistribution. Here again, Hurston's words offer a fitting warning to those who would rectify the injustices of the past with the politics of the present: "There has been no proof in the world so far that you would be less arrogant if you held the lever of power in your hands."[10]

15

Hulu's *1619* Docuseries Peddles False History

Following the release of the book-length expansion of the 1619 Project, Nikole Hannah-Jones began converting selected chapters into a six-episode documentary for the Hulu streaming service. At the time of the series premiere in early 2023, I was invited by Reason Magazine *and the* New York Post *to prepare a scholarly assessment of its historical claims. The first episode in the series features an adaptation of Hannah-Jones's opening chapter, including an exploration of her contested claims about the American Revolution. As she did in the book, Hannah-Jones repeated and further exaggerated her original argument linking the revolutionary cause to the defense of slavery. The Hulu series sets these claims against the visual backdrop of colonial history sites in Virginia even though, as I soon discovered, Hannah-Jones and her guests misrepresented the events that took place at these locations.*

This episode contains some of Hannah-Jones's most detailed explorations of her claims, including a lengthy interview with historian Woody Holton. It also takes the greatest liberties to date with the evidentiary record. In particular, Hannah-Jones attempted to rehabilitate the reputation of Lord Dunmore, the last Royalist governor of Virginia, by depicting him as an agent of emancipation against the slave-owning Americans. In my essay I investigate the Dunmore thesis in detail and show that Hannah-Jones altered the timeline of the relevant events while also obscuring Dunmore's own active participation in plantation slavery. The resulting episode further ex-

126 | *The 1619 Project Myth*

aggerates the historical errors and misrepresentations of the book and newspaper versions of the 1619 Project.

THE NEW YORK TIMES'S 1619 Project selected Colonial Williamsburg, Virginia, as a filming location for its new Hulu docuseries. In doing so, creator Nikole Hannah-Jones sought to bolster her project's most troublesome claim—the assertion that British overtures toward emancipation impelled the American colonists into revolution, ultimately securing an independent United States.

In the past three years, the *Times* has grappled with the fallout from Hannah-Jones's assertion,[1] including the revelation that it ignored its own fact-checker's warnings against printing the charge. The *Times* tempered its language to apply to "some of" the colonists, only to see it reasserted by Hannah-Jones in her public commentaries. Later, a related line about the project's goal of replacing 1776 with a "true founding" of 1619 disappeared without notice from the *Times*'s website.

The newspaper found itself in a balancing act between its writer's uncompromising positions and the need to preserve credibility as it made a Pulitzer Prize bid with the series. But Hannah-Jones was not ready to abandon the claim at the center of her lead essay, and the first episode of the Hulu series makes that abundantly clear.

The scene opens in Williamsburg on the grounds of its reconstructed colonial Governor's Palace, where Hannah-Jones joins University of South Carolina professor Woody Holton—one of a handful of heterodox historians who defended the 1619 Project's original narrative. As the cameras pan across streets filled with historical reenactors and tourists in front of restored colonial buildings, the pair take another stab at resurrecting the 1619 Project's narrative about the American Revolution.

The evidence that a British threat to slavery impelled Virginians—or perhaps "the colonists" at large, in Hannah-Jones's imprecise phrasing—to revolt may be found in the November 1775 decree of John Murray, fourth earl of Dunmore, Virginia's last Royalist governor. Facing the collapse of British rule, Dunmore announced that any enslaved male from a household in rebellion would be granted freedom in exchange for military service on the British side.

Hulu's 1619 Docuseries Peddles False History | 127

Dunmore's decree made him the author of an "Emancipation Proclamation" of sorts, both Hannah-Jones and Holton contend. Their language intentionally evokes parallels to President Abraham Lincoln's famous order freeing the slaves of the rebellious Confederacy in 1863.

Prompted by Hannah-Jones's questioning, Holton then recounts his version of the lesser-known events of some four score and eight years prior. "Dunmore issued that Emancipation Proclamation November 1775," he explains, "and that Emancipation Proclamation infuriated white southerners."

We see the visual power of the Hulu production at this moment as Holton lifts his finger, pointing at the Governor's Palace, the centerpiece of the Colonial Williamsburg historical park. The camera quickly shifts to the re-created structure as he begins to speak.

"Because this building is supposed to symbolize white rule over blacks, and now the guy inhabiting that building," Dunmore, "has turned things upside down and is leading blacks against whites."

Hannah-Jones interjects, "So you have this situation where many Virginians and other southern colonists—they're not really convinced that they want to side with the patriots. And this turns many of them towards the revolution. Is that right?"

Holton answers without a flinch. "If you ask them, it did. The record is absolutely clear."

The scene is an authoritatively delivered pronouncement set to stunning cinematography, but it's also false history.

At the time of his decree, the real Dunmore had not set foot in Williamsburg in almost five months. His order, decreeing martial law in the colony and calling on slaves to enlist in a Royalist militia, came not from the governor's residence but from a position of exile aboard HMS *William*, a naval ship anchored off the coast of Norfolk, Virginia.

Dunmore abandoned the Governor's Palace on June 8, 1775, amid signs that patriot militiamen were converging on Williamsburg to defend the House of Burgesses from a threatened power grab by the crown. The trouble began a few weeks earlier with a botched attempt by Dunmore to seize the colony's gunpowder stores as a preemptive strike against revolutionary grumblings.

Indeed, when Dunmore fled the capital, he carried away a sizable staff of "servants" from the palace grounds and relocated them to Porto Bello, his sprawling plantation a few miles up the river.

Yes, the 1619 Project's designated agent of "emancipation" for the British crown was an enslaver himself. Dunmore encamped on a succession of warships anchored in the nearby York River, never to return to the building where Holton erroneously situated the decree. He occasionally took a barge over to the plantation house at Porto Bello to enjoy fine dining with his officers, served by his relocated slaves. But that ended as patriot militias gained control of the peninsula on which the property sat, and Dunmore withdrew to Norfolk.

By November 7, 1775—the date of the order—he had long lost any semblance of control over the colony. The decree anticipated an unsuccessful campaign to regain a foothold in the colony. In retrospect, it was a desperate move to restore himself to power by inducing a slave revolt amid the already-unfolding revolution, rather than any true attempt to effect "emancipation" at large.

The inescapable progression of the timeline has always worked against Hannah-Jones's narrative. Leaning heavily on Holton's academic work, she asserts that Dunmore galvanized the southern colonies against Britain by imperiling their slave plantations and moving them into the revolutionary column.

Holton's commentaries in the docuseries signal his concurrence with this view insofar as it relates to Virginia, even as he stops short of Hannah-Jones's blurry ascription of this motive to "the colonists" of the future United States at large. Yet as a matter of history, it collides with easily documented facts.

As the events around Williamsburg revealed, Dunmore's order was a reaction to—not a cause of—a revolution already in full swing. The road to American independence began in Massachusetts over a decade earlier with men such as James Otis (incidentally, an early abolitionist) rallying against the crown under the banner of "no taxation without representation." Virginia expressed solidarity with this cause long before Dunmore's order.

In 1774, the House of Burgesses adopted a resolution of fasting to show their support for the people of Boston, then under a punitive edict from London in retaliation for its tax protests. A short time later, a group of leading Virginians, including George Washington and George Mason, signed the Fairfax Resolves, stating a long list of grievances against the crown (its promotion of the slave trade among them) and rejecting parliamentary control over the colonies.

Patrick Henry, another Virginian, delivered his famous "Give me liberty, or give me death" speech in March 1775 before Dunmore even uttered a word about enlisting slaves. Washington himself would take command of the Continental Army on June 19, 1775, organizing his troops in New England after the Battle of Bunker Hill.

As his shipbound circumstances illustrated, the remnants of Lord Dunmore's governorship amounted to little more than paper when he issued his decree that autumn. It is undoubtedly true that Dunmore's order further inflamed an already-raging revolution, including nudging some slave-owning planters off the fence. But its sweeping martial law provision was likely the greater source of outrage.

As Dunmore's own financial interests illustrate, he had every intention of honoring the decree's explicit exemptions for the human property of Royalist enslavers. None of these complicating details receive even the slightest amount of attention in the Hulu presentation from Williamsburg.

Hannah-Jones's latest chronological mishap adds to a long list of errors that have plagued the 1619 Project. In this instance, it also speaks to a deeper underlying negligence around matters of basic fact.

As a flashpoint of controversy since the 1619 Project's inception, the claims about slavery in the American Revolution warranted careful attention. The docuseries offered Hannah-Jones yet another opportunity to clarify her case, ostensibly with the guidance of trained historians such as Holton. Instead, she pushed ahead, unaware of a timeline that any tour guide at the Governor's Palace could have resolved for her.

Holton's case is a bit more complicated, as his academic works, including his 2021 book *Liberty Is Sweet*, evince awareness of Dunmore's shipbound circumstances after his June 1775 flight. In fact, Holton's scholarly publications have attempted to walk a fine line around the 1619 Project that chafes with his ringing public endorsements of the same in popular media.

A revealing footnote tucked inside *Liberty Is Sweet* states that Hannah-Jones "vastly exaggerates the size and strength of the British abolition movement" in the years before the revolution, dampening her attempts to use the 1772 anti-slavery *Somerset* case as an instigating cause of American independence.[2]

Yet as the docuseries shows, it is Holton who assigns particular significance to the filming location in Williamsburg, and it is Holton who points to the governor's residence as the source of his own vastly exaggerated "Emancipation Proclamation."

This peculiar convergence of factual error and cinematic misdirection comes with an ironic twist. If there are historical parallels to be drawn between Dunmore's order and later events, it is not Lincoln's Emancipation Proclamation but rather the desperate actions of his Confederate adversaries.

In the waning days of the Civil War, Jefferson Davis authorized what became known as General Orders No. 14. The measure called for the "enlistment of colored persons" into the Confederate army, with provisions to accept any male slave "with his own consent and with the approbation of his master by a written instrument conferring, as he may, the rights of a freedman" in exchange for service.[3] The Confederates paraded a handful of black companies on the streets of Richmond in late March 1865. Some of these troops were likely involved in a rearguard skirmish as Robert E. Lee's army abandoned the city and made its fateful retreat toward Appomattox Courthouse.

The Confederates' measure was no act of magnanimity by the slavers, but rather an exercise in desperation by a government on the precipice of collapse. Like Dunmore some 90 years before him, Davis lost his seat of power and found his forces in disarray. Most historians interpret his actions in this panicked context, not as some sudden change of heart on the central issue that sparked the Civil War.

And yet a parallel scenario from the American Revolution is now being touted as proof of a long-forgotten British anti-slavery crusade?

We may look on in amazement, amusement, and disgust as the 1619 Project's creator and its academic boosters attempt a peculiar rehabilitation of Dunmore—enslaver, plantation master, and Royalist autocrat—as a leading and even celebrated agent of emancipation.

16

The 1619 Project's Confusion on Capitalism

In August 2019, I penned the first scholarly criticism of Matthew Desmond's 1619 Project contribution on "capitalism," appearing in National Review *a few days after the project itself came out in print. When Hulu converted the topic of Desmond's essay into a full episode of its documentary miniseries,* National Review *again asked me to provide an expert assessment of the episode's claims about the economics of slavery.*

Curiously, Desmond did not appear in this Hulu episode. Hannah-Jones filled in, presenting most of his arguments as her own. As in the other episodes, Hannah-Jones made no effort to address the factual deficiencies of Desmond's original essay or its extended version from the book. She simply swapped out a few of his claimed examples of slavery's economic legacy in the present day. In place of Desmond's attempts to connect Microsoft Excel to plantation accounting books, Hannah-Jones imputes the same false lineage to Amazon warehouses.

The episode's overt embrace of radical left-wing economic doctrines might be its most distinctive feature. Just as Desmond's book chapter revision appended socialist theorizing to his anti-capitalist narrative, the "Capitalism" Hulu episode brought in experts drawn exclusively from the academic far left. Hannah-Jones's guests included Seth Rockman, a polemicist associated with the beleaguered New History of Capitalism school's resuscitation of the King Cotton thesis of American economic development, and Robin D. G. Kelley, a Marxist historian who defines mainstream economics as inherently "exploitative."

In their respective performances, each academic recited anti-capitalist platitudes and repeated earlier semantic appeals concerning the definition of capitalism. Evidence, by contrast, was nowhere to be found, although this absence was to be expected, as Hannah-Jones long ago abandoned any semblance of anchoring her arguments in historical sources and data. The resulting episode symptomizes the transformation of the 1619 Project into an exclusively political endeavor in which historical interpretations are evaluated not for the strength or weakness of their evidence, but for their utility in promoting economic redistribution in the present day.

A PERVASIVE SENSE of confusion characterizes Hulu's 1619 Project episode "Capitalism," beginning with the basic definition of its titular term. Project creator Nikole Hannah-Jones opens the episode by conceding that "I don't feel like most of us actually know what capitalism means." This should have provided her an opportunity for self-reflection on how the embattled project has, over the last three years, trudged its way through the economic dimensions of slavery.

The original *New York Times* version of the project assigned the topic to Princeton sociologist Matthew Desmond, a novice without any scholarly expertise or methodological training in one of economic history's most thoroughly scrutinized topics.[1] The resulting essay blended empirical error with a basic misreading of the academic literature to almost comical ends. He casually repeated a thoroughly debunked statistical claim from a "New History of Capitalism" (NHC) scholar, Ed Baptist,[2] who erroneously attributes the growth of the antebellum cotton industry's crop yield to the increased beating of slaves (it was actually due to improved seed technology).[3] At one point, Desmond even asserted a lineal descent from plantation accounting books to Microsoft Excel—the result of misreading a passage in another book that explicitly disavowed this same connection.

Desmond is conspicuously absent from the new Hulu episode, although Amazon warehouses do apparently supplant Microsoft as the modern-day iteration of plantation economics—a message repeatedly emphasized as the camera shots flash between historical photographs of slaves working in the cotton fields of the antebellum South and footage of an Amazon distribution center. The cinematic juxtaposition is intended to provoke. Instead, it simply ventures into morally offensive analogy, stripped of any sense of proportion or understanding of slavery's abject brutality. Though she stops just short of saying as much, Hannah-Jones wishes for her viewers to identify an hourly wage job with the internet retail giant as a modern "capitalist" continuation of chattel slavery.

And thus, we return to the matter of definitions. Seeking a succinct explanation of "capitalism," Hannah-Jones first consults historian Seth Rockman of Brown University. Rockman is an unusual choice, not only as a fellow traveler of Baptist's embattled NHC school but for his own definitional confusions about the same term. He wrote a widely referenced 2014 article asserting that the NHC "has minimal investment in a fixed or theoretical definition of capitalism" while simultaneously insisting that slavery is "integral, rather than oppositional, to capitalism."[4] Capitalism cannot even be defined, but it is definitionally wedded to slavery. And so goes Rockman's answer in the docuseries. After brushing aside a common dictionary's association of the term with "a system of private property in which the free market coordinates buyers and sellers," he settles on "it's not really clear." Nonetheless, capitalism, in his mind, still clearly encompasses slavery, with no further explanation needed.

Hannah-Jones's semantic exercise shifts as she brings in a new consultant to the 1619 Project, UCLA historian Robin D. G. Kelley. Unlike Rockman's self-contradictory equivocation, Kelley minces no words: "The reality is that capitalism is based on the exploitation of labor. It's that simple." And with that assertion, the 1619 Project episode further stumbles through its investigation of "capitalism" by adopting an unvarnished Marxist conceptualization of the term.

Equating capitalism with the exploitation of workers certainly serves the purpose of designating chattel slavery as a capitalistic institution, but it is simply not an accurate—or even functional—definition of the concept. Ancient Roman slavery, medieval feudalism, Soviet-era gulags, and North Korean prison camps today would also qualify as "capitalism" if we reduce the concept to exploitative worker conditions, and indeed that is how Hannah-Jones, under Kelley's aggressively ideological guidance, proceeds.

From this dubious starting point, Hannah-Jones then opens the floodgates for almost every economic fallacy and pejorative denigration imaginable to

134 | *The 1619 Project Myth*

describe economic development under market-based capitalism. Aided by Rockman, Hannah-Jones begins in palpable circularity by assuming the very premise she purports to demonstrate. American slavery "can never be separated from the history of capitalism," Rockman tells us, resting this claim on the banal observation that slave-produced goods were bought and sold outside of the slaveholding regions and were used in economic production all over the world. The same reductionist logic could be used to deem the entire modern American economy a simple appendage of the economic system of China, Venezuela, or any other autocratic regime with which we trade or have financial entanglements. Yet the simple presence of trade, exchange, and financial institutions is not exclusive to capitalism. These have been features of almost every society in human history, free and unfree.

Seeking to drive home Rockman's point, Hannah-Jones informs her viewers that slave-produced cotton accounted for more than half of all U.S. exports before the Civil War. The number is accurate for the period after 1820, but the claim lacks perspective. In the antebellum period, total U.S. export volume never exceeded 7 percent of GDP. As economist Gavin Wright notes, "The chief sources of U.S. growth were domestic."[5] In this same period, Wright shows, the American South was a diminishing market compared to the rest of the country. The share of total income arising from the southern states dropped from 57.4 percent on the eve of the American Revolution in 1774 to just 30.5 percent in 1860 at the outbreak of secessionism. Immigration patterns favored the free states in this era, and the Civil War itself provided a real-time demonstration of the industrialized North's superior economic position vis-à-vis an underdeveloped South. Business with slave owners undoubtedly implicated some northern banks and financial institutions in the practice, but did they "create [the] entire financial industry in the nascent United States" as Hannah-Jones purports? Only if one double-counts intermediate transactions to exaggerate the magnitude of slavery's economic reach until it includes the lion's share of economic output.[6] In the NHC literature, no relevant adjustments are made to the remainder of the economy outside of the roughly 5–6 percent of antebellum GDP tied up in cotton production.

The docuseries episode nonetheless proceeds from the NHC literature's faulty empirical assumptions, unencumbered by any need to show its math. "If you don't have slave-grown cotton, you don't have an American industrial revolution," Rockman declares. "It's as simple as that." And yet economic reality is anything but simple. History provides numerous examples—Canada, Japan, several European states—of economies that underwent massive industrialization in the 19th century without the alleged benefits of slavery. It also offers examples such as Brazil, which maintained a large slave economy for several decades longer than the United States did without industrializing. Indeed, one empirical analysis of U.S. economic growth over time reveals that counties with slavery lagged behind free-labor regions long after slavery's abolition.[7] The plantation system may have enriched a small, elite group of slave owners during its existence, but slavery is unambiguously harmful to economic development in the long run.

Economists have long rejected the class of monocausal development theories that purport to find the economic engine of an entire epoch in a single good or product, such as oil or railroads in more recent times. Aside from seldom exceeding single-digit shares of economic output, one-industry theories of economic development must contend with the counterfactual presented by the allegedly dominant industry's closest substitutes. In the case of cotton, alternative sources could be found outside of the American South—and indeed they were during the Civil War, when the blockade induced the textile mills of Europe to turn to Egypt, India, and South America for their raw materials. In this respect, the 1619 Project repeats the same economic error that led the Confederacy to mistakenly proclaim that "cotton is king," assuming none would dare make war upon its plantation system for risk of amputating the alleged source of their own wealth.[8] In practice, King Cotton was but a garish pretender to an economic throne that did not even exist.

Although the 1619 Project's anti-capitalism arises from ideological roots, it is difficult to avoid the conclusion that the series's elementary misrepresentations of American economic history arise from the abject ignorance of its creator and her chosen guests. A revealing moment occurs shortly after their botched foray into economic statistics, with Hannah-Jones declaring that "the education I received has long said that slavery wasn't profitable." Rockman appends a conspiratorial twist, asserting that American society "has very aggressively tried to erase those connections."

The unprofitability thesis traces back to the turn-of-the-century writings of historian Ulrich Bonnell Phillips, who depicted slavery as a declining in-

136 | *The 1619 Project Myth*

stitution on the eve of the Civil War. Phillips's argument was conclusively debunked back in 1958 by economists Alfred Conrad and John R. Meyer, who used plantation records to show that slavery was profitable at the time of its abolition.[9] Hannah-Jones and Rockman, therefore, build their case against an obsolete theory that few academics have taken seriously in over 60 years. Furthermore, Phillips's position was almost certainly not being taught with any regularity in universities by the 1990s, when each completed their undergraduate studies in history. As with much of the NHC literature, the 1619 Project's derivative interpretation of slavery emerges from a branch of the academy that has chosen to isolate itself from most modern scholarly works on the economics of slavery, even as it advances an unfounded assertion of its own novelty.

The ideological core of the series's "Capitalism" episode, however, is based not on NHC literature but rather on a droning foray into Marxist theorizing. Kelley, the project's newest contributor, hails from an idiosyncratic branch of the communist philosopher's followers, as filtered through an explicitly racial lens. Hannah-Jones summarizes his take about halfway through the episode when she states that "capitalism is designed to exploit labor and human beings, but all people are not exploited equally." Race explains the difference in exploitative severity that each laborer faces. Kelley's explication on this point is little more than muddled aphorism, with a string of circular declamations simply asserting that "racial capitalism is capitalism—they're one and the same." The viewer is left to make the next deduction, namely that capitalism itself is inherently racist and therefore deserving to be jettisoned.

Racial exploitation also functions as Kelley's theoretical fix to a conundrum of the Marxist world. Marx famously predicted that the numerical advantages of the proletariat classes would eventually allow them to rise and seize the means of production from the capitalists. In practice, true proletarian revolutions seldom materialize. Instead, most Marxian socialist regimes get their start from small, violent bands of left-wing ideologues staging coups.[10] Other branches of Marxist theory have retrofitted self-serving explanations into this gap, usually either faulting capitalists for obstructing class-based collective action or appointing themselves as a vanguard to usher in a broader socialist movement.

The 1619 Project takes a different route, starting with Desmond's essay in the book version of the series. The failure of labor to collectively assert itself in the United States, Desmond alleges, is due to the capitalists' using racial division to segment the working class. "As Northern elites were forging an industrial proletariat of factory workers," he explains, "Southern elites . . . began creating an agrarian proletariat," and never the twain shall meet on the revolutionary picket lines. As Kelley elaborates in the Hulu episode, "white workers choose racial solidarity over their own economic interest" and accordingly undermine the organizing mechanism of the proletarian whole, the labor union.

At this point the episode thrusts itself into a political crusade to unionize an Amazon warehouse in Bessemer, Alabama, bringing the narrative full circle. If Amazon is the modern successor to the slave plantation, and Amazon workers sharply divide during several successive votes to unionize, as happened at the Bessemer facility,[11] then the outcome cannot possibly reflect the triumph of any legitimate argument against unions. It must be "racial capitalism," separating the workers from their scientifically discerned collective labor interests and leading some of them into the service of their own capitalist exploiters.

Hannah-Jones cannot help but see this batty narrative lurking behind every single setback to the Amazon unionization organizers, whose cause she advances as self-evidently sacrosanct. Indeed, the United States' relatively low rates of union membership become their own evidence that an exploitative "racial capitalism" has thoroughly corrupted our labor market. "For the last 40 years we've experienced a kind of onslaught against labor," Kelley asserts.

Hannah-Jones nods in agreement, volunteering her own declarative assessment that unionization and civil rights are synonymous causes. In doing so, she repeats what historian Paul Moreno dubs "one of the hoariest myths in the history of the American labor movement"[12]—the notion that racial animus is externally imposed on the working class to keep it divided and weak. In reality, the long history of unionization in the United States is replete with homegrown racism, as organized labor has sought to increase white workers' wages by driving African-Americans out of the competitive workforce. Many early-20th-century union initiatives, including working-hour restrictions, minimum wages, and collectively codified seniority privileges for existing workers, allowed organizers to cartelize white labor against wage competition from African-Americans and immigrants. The mostly white union sector benefited from artificially higher pay under these measures, whereas blacks found themselves excluded from employment entirely.

Even as some African-Americans attempted to unionize separately during this era, with varying degrees of success, many civil rights leaders recognized organized labor as a bulwark of institutional racism. A 1930s National Association for the Advancement of Colored People (NAACP) publication declared that the Wagner Act, a pro-union measure from the New Deal, was "fraught with grave danger to Negro labor" because it "empowers organized labor to exclude from employment in any industry all workers who do not belong to a union."[13] Since many unions in this era excluded non-white members entirely and others maintained soft discriminatory practices, the "closed shop" provisions of the act would effectively bar black workers from entire companies and industries. Writing almost a century later, Hannah-Jones looks past the overt racism that plagues the history of the American labor movement. To her, "right to work" laws are nefarious tools of racial-economic oppression, in contrast with the 1930s, "when the U.S. had one of the highest unionization rates in the world." This rosy picture of a unionized golden age is not only in direct conflict with the position of the New Deal–era NAACP, it also contradicts Hannah-Jones's own statements in a different episode of the Hulu series in which she acknowledges the discriminatory effects of the Wagner Act as part of her case for reparations.

Returning to Kelley, we find an answer as to why this historical omission of organized labor's racism is made in the "Capitalism" episode, but not in the others. The Marxist academic is best known for his heterodox history of the "long civil rights movement," the thesis of which is that the Communist Party during the 1930s was among the most important organizations for the African-American civil rights cause.[14] Kelley comes from a far-left intellectual tradition that traces its roots to the late-life work of W. E. B. Du Bois, when the famous black intellectual split from the avowedly anti-communist leadership of the NAACP.[15]

Du Bois, in turn, spent his final years gallivanting with Mao Zedong[16] and touting the alleged credentials of Joseph Stalin as a leading anti-racist.[17] But there's an older radical tradition undergirding this line of reasoning and the NHC literature more generally. Desmond's print version of the "racial capitalism" thesis openly ponders why American industrialization didn't follow the course that "Karl Marx and a long list of other political theorists predicted," namely "the formation of a Labor Party or even ushering in a socialist revolution." This "new" take on capitalism's history is really the repackaging of a stale thesis. It traces back to the German philosopher Werner Sombart, himself an adherent of a branch of Marxian heterodoxy (and later a collaborator with National Socialism), who observed in 1906 that "the Negro question has directly removed any class character from each of the two [American political] parties."[18] This split allegedly rendered both unable to serve as a locus of labor organizing. And in Desmond's telling, the resulting weakening of laboring-class consciousness is the real economic legacy of slavery—a legacy he sees manifest today in every defeat that the far left incurs at the ballot box.

In the 1619 Project's peculiar political economy, slavery is the root of the American electorate's resistance to Piketty-style wealth taxes. It's also the reason we don't have a fully socialized health care system, why the IRS doesn't hire enough auditors, and why the Green New Deal has thus far failed to advance through Congress. The Hulu episode adds one more political grievance to the list. Slavery, we learn, is also why Amazon warehouses remain insufficiently unionized.

The historical evidence behind each of these claims is thin at best; it more often consists of NHC scholars venturing beyond their own competencies while attempting to interpret complex events in economic history. As with the NHC scholars' hapless rehabilitation of the "King Cotton" theory, the Amazon narrative unintentionally evokes late-antebellum-era defenses of slavery, namely that wage earners were "free but in name—the slaves of endless toil," to quote the slaver-poet and politician William J. Grayson.[19] But the Hulu series has made it abundantly clear that history is no longer the primary purpose of the 1619 Project, assuming it ever was.

The informed viewer cannot help but notice an element of accident in Hannah-Jones's economic misadventures. Progressive policy aims characterized the 1619 Project from the beginning, to be sure, but its confused economics left the project's creator adrift in a sea of withering criticism.[20] As she cast about for new sources to salvage her narrative, she eventually landed in the fringes of academic Marxism. But there is no reason for outrage over the many errors of fact and economic reasoning that result from this witless embrace of anti-capitalist crankery. The incoherent narrative that the 1619

Project builds in its attempt to link modern Amazon warehouses to slavery offers no meaningful insights about the history or economic workings of either institution. But it is sufficiently self-discrediting to dissuade most viewers outside of the already converted.

17

The Tooth-Fairy Economics of Slavery Reparations

This piece was co-authored with David R. Henderson.

The final episode of the 1619 Project Hulu miniseries concludes with a rousing call for a national slavery reparations program. In making this call, Nikole Hannah-Jones demonstrates the overt political evolution of her project's historical narrative. America's past has become her tool for reparations advocacy in the present.

Whatever position one might take on slavery reparations, its execution would entail extreme budgetary outlays and associated economic disruptions. When presented with these challenges, Hannah-Jones has taken to dismissing them with little more than a wave of the hand. The concluding episode of the Hulu series follows this course by appealing to fringe economic doctrines and essentially proposing a blank check for reparations without any real plan to pay for the program.

Shortly after the final Hulu episode appeared, I collaborated with economist David R. Henderson to investigate the economic repercussions of Hannah-Jones's proposal at face value. Without taking a stance on the normative questions around reparations, we limited ourselves to evaluating the repercussions of its proposed $13 trillion price tag. As we show, this impractical scheme would either necessitate completely reallocating the bulk of the federal budget to this new program, or financing it through money creation at levels that would almost certainly trigger an unprecedented inflationary crisis. In the *final assessment, the 1619 Project's flagship policy prescription has no viable economic path to implementation.*

THE REPARATIONS MOVEMENT has gained tremendous ground in recent years by offering promises of compensation to the descendants of slavery's victims in the United States. The proposal forms the centerpiece of the *New York Times* 1619 Project, which is now a multimillion-dollar docuseries on the Hulu streaming service. A reparations task force in San Francisco recently recommended $5 million payments to African-American residents, and several Democratic members of Congress have pressed the Biden administration to prioritize the same cause at the federal level. Reparations have even made their way into children's programming, with a recent episode of the Disney cartoon *The Proud Family* depicting them, angrily and self-righteously, as society's obligation to African-Americans.

The rhetoric around these proposals often adopts a moralizing tone about restitution for past injustices, many of which are all too real. As a matter of economics, though, reparations advocates offer surprisingly little in the way of viable solutions. If the U.S. government tried to implement the reparations program that the 1619 Project espouses, we would get huge increases in both taxes and inflation. Yet the key economist advising on this proposal denies that any taxes would have to increase.

In the climactic conclusion to the Hulu series, 1619 Project creator Nikole Hannah-Jones explains that the demand for "reparations is not just about slavery, but about decades of government-backed legal apartheid deployed against the descendants of the enslaved." As we pointed out in the *Wall Street Journal* on February 22, 2023, "almost every example presented is the result of government policies that, in purpose or effect, discriminated against African-Americans."[1] The particular interventions we highlighted were eminent domain, racial redlining of mortgages, and enforcement of union monopolies that excluded black people.

But the only remedy for the mislabeled track record of government-inflicted injustice, viewers are told, is a massive government redistribution program with a price tag of $13 trillion. Let's put this in perspective in two ways. First, $13 trillion is over half of current U.S. GDP. Second, it amounts to $312,000 per black man, woman, and child. If you gasp at San Francisco's

The Tooth-Fairy Economics of Slavery Reparations | 143

$5 million and think $312,000 is no big deal, realize that $310,000 in reparations per person, multiplied by about 41.6 million African-Americans, is quite a big deal.

Ms. Hannah-Jones interviews Duke University economist William A. Darity, one of the most prominent academic voices behind the $13 trillion number. Darity has advanced similar dollar amounts in his scholarly work, including a 2022 article in the *Journal of Economic Perspectives*.[2] As with the Hulu episode, he offers this figure while eliding difficult questions about financing this redistributive payout.

Vaguely sensing that there's no such thing as a free lunch, Hannah-Jones asks where the federal government would get the money to pay such a massive amount. Wouldn't taxes have to be raised? she queries. Mr. Darity confidently asserts that no such action is necessary.

"It's a matter of the federal government financing it in the same way that it financed . . . the stimulus package for the Great Recession" and the COVID-era CARES Act, Darity continues. To do so, the federal government need only "spend the money but without raising taxes."

This verges on tooth-fairy economics.

The cold reality of public finance means that every government outlay must be paid eventually, whether through taxes in the present; higher inflation, which is also a tax; or higher taxes on future generations. The federal government has no good option when it comes to just "spending the money."

If the Federal Reserve monetized the whole amount, base money, which is currency in circulation plus bank reserves, would increase by $13 trillion. M2, the conventional measure of the money supply, is 3.96 times the monetary base. If that relationship held, then increasing the monetary base by $13 trillion would increase M2 by 3.96 times $13 trillion, which is $51 trillion. M2 is currently $21 trillion; $51 trillion is a whopping 245 percent increase. So if the spending occurred all in one year, inflation would be about 240 percent. Critical Race Theory would unite with Modern Monetary Theory in an inflationary spiral.

What if the Fed didn't buy any of the new debt? Then future taxpayers would be on the hook. In a given year, the federal government raises about $4.8 trillion in revenues. So paying off just the new $13 trillion debt would require almost three years of federal revenue.

144 | *The 1619 Project Myth*

The only other alternative to increasing current taxes, creating massive inflation, or increasing future taxes would be to enact massive cuts in other programs. Remember earlier this month when, in his State of the Union address, President Biden accused congressional Republicans of wanting to sunset Social Security and Medicare? If the $13 trillion reparations were paid, sunsetting those programs, or reining them in by a double-digit percent, would almost certainly be on the table.

Almost everyone who designed the government's discriminatory programs is long gone from office; most are dead, as are all plantation owners who perpetrated the original atrocities of slavery. So the vast majority of people who would shoulder the financial burden of reparations are people who had nothing to do with either slavery or the century of discriminatory policies that followed.

How about instead going through the various federal programs, and state and local programs, for that matter, that intervene in markets or violate property rights, often in discriminatory ways, and ending them? It would be great if Nikole Hannah-Jones and William Darity signed on to this project in the modern era.

Notes

1. How the 1619 Project Rehabilitates the "King Cotton" Thesis

1. Nunn, Nathan. 2008. "Slavery, Inequality, and Economic Development in the Americas: An Examination of the Engerman-Sokoloff Hypothesis." In *Institutions and Economic Performance*, ed. E Helpmann, 148–180. Cambridge, MA: Harvard University Press.

2. See chapter herein entitled "The Statistical Errors of the Reparations Agenda."

3. Olmstead, Alan L., and Paul W. Rhode. 2018. "Cotton, Slavery, and the New History of Capitalism." *Explorations in Economic History*, January.

4. Hannah-Jones, Nikole. 2019. "Economists dispute a few of Baptist's calculations but not the book itself nor its thesis." Twitter, August 18. https://twitter.com/nhannah-jones/status/1163030801778401281

5. Murray, J., A. Olmstead, T. Logan, J. Pritchett, and P. Rousseau. 2015. "Roundtable of Reviews for 'The Half Has Never Been Told: Slavery and the Making of American Capitalism' by Edward E. Baptist." *The Journal of Economic History*, 75(3): 919–931.

6. Hilt, Eric. 2017. "Economic History, Historical Analysis, and the 'New History of Capitalism.'" *The Journal of Economic History*, 77(2): 511–536.

7. Engerman, Stanley L. 2017. "Review of 'The Business of Slavery and the Rise of American Capitalism, 1815–1860' by Calvin Schermerhorn and 'The Half Has Never Been Told: Slavery and the Making of American Capitalism' by Edward E. Baptist." *Journal of Economic Literature*, 55(2): 637–643.

8. Fitzhugh, George. 1857. *Cannibals All! Or, Slaves Without Masters* (electronic ed.). Richmond, VA: A. Morris, Publisher.

2. The Anti-Capitalist Ideology of Slavery

1. Fitzhugh, George. 1854. *Sociology for the South, or The Failure of Free Society* (electronic ed.). Richmond, VA: A. Morris, Publisher.

2. Fitzhugh, George. 1861. "The Times and The War." *De Bow's Review*, 31(1): 1–13.

3. Desmond, Matthew. 2019. "American Capitalism Is Brutal. You Can Trace That to the Plantation." *The New York Times Magazine*, August 14.

4. Olmstead, Alan L., and Paul W. Rhode. 2018. "Cotton, Slavery, and the New History of Capitalism." *Explorations in Economic History*, January.

146 | *Notes*

5. See chapter herein entitled "The Statistical Errors of the Reparations Agenda"; Baptist, Edward E. 2014. *The Half Has Never Been Told: Slavery and the Making of American Capitalism*. New York: Basic Books.

6. Fitzhugh, George. 1857. *Cannibals All! Or, Slaves Without Masters* (electronic ed.). Richmond, VA: A. Morris, Publisher.

7. Levy, David M., and Sandra J. Peart. 2001. "The Secret History of the Dismal Science. Part 1: Economics, Religion, and Race in the 19th Century." *The Library of Economics and Liberty*, January 22.

3. How Capitalist-Abolitionists Fought Slavery

1. Magness, Phillip W. 2019. "William Leggett: Free Trade, Hard Money, and Abolitionism." *Online Library of Liberty*, July.

2. *New Method of Assorting the Mail, as Practised by Southern Slave-Holders, or Attack on the Post Office*. 1853. Charleston, South Carolina.

3. Grinder, Brian, and Dan Cooper. 2017. "Spies, Abolitionists and the Origins of Credit Rating Agencies." *Financial History* (Winter): 10–11, 38.

4. Foulke, a vice president of Dun & Bradstreet, was also an early benefactor of the American Institute for Economic Research (AIER) and a friend of E. C. Harwood. Foulke, Roy Anderson. 1896. *The Sinews of American Commerce*.

5. Letter and envelope from L. Tappan to Lysander Spooner. 1855. New York Heritage Digital Collections. November 21.

6. See chapter herein entitled "The Statistical Errors of the Reparations Agenda"; Olmstead, Alan L., and Paul W. Rhode. 2018. "Cotton, Slavery, and the New History of Capitalism." *Explorations in Economic History*, January; see chapter herein entitled "A Comment on the 'New' History of American Capitalism."

7. See chapter herein entitled "The Anti-Capitalist Ideology of Slavery."

4. The Statistical Errors of the Reparations Agenda

1. Paschal, Olivia, and Madeleine Carlisle. 2019. "Read Ta-Nehisi Coates's Testimony on Reparations." *The Atlantic*, June 19.

2. Baptist, Edward E. 2014. *The Half Has Never Been Told: Slavery and the Making of American Capitalism*. New York: Basic Books.

3. Hansen, Bradley A. 2014. "The Back of Ed Baptist's Envelope." *Bradley A. Hansen's Blog*, October 30. http://bradleyahansen.blogspot.com/2014/10/the-back-of-ed-baptists-envelope.html

4. Olmstead, Alan L., and Paul W. Rhode. 2018. "Cotton, Slavery, and the New History of Capitalism." *Explorations in Economic History*, January.

5. Fogel, Robert William, and Stanley L. Engerman. 1995. *Time on the Cross: The Economics of American Negro Slavery*, vol. 1. W. W. Norton & Company; Engerman, Stanley L. 2017. "Review of 'The Business of Slavery and the Rise of American Capitalism, 1815–1860' by Calvin Schermerhorn and 'The Half Has Never Been Told: Slavery and the Making of American Capitalism' by Edward E. Baptist." *Journal of Economic Literature*, 55(2): 637–643.

Notes | 147

6. Anderson, Carol. 2016. *White Rage: The Unspoken Truth of Our Racial Divide*. New York: Bloomsbury.

7. Drescher, Seymour. 2010. *Econocide: British Slavery in the Era of Abolition*, 2nd ed., xiix. Chapel Hill: University of North Carolina Press.

8. Fitzhugh, George. 1857. *Cannibals All! Or, Slaves Without Masters* (electronic ed.). Richmond, VA: A. Morris, Publisher. https://docsouth.unc.edu/southlit/fitzhughcan/fitzcan.html at p. 79; Levy, David M., and Sandra J. Peart. 2001. "The Secret History of the Dismal Science. Part 1: Economics, Religion and Race in the 19th Century." *The Library of Economics and Liberty*, January 22.

5. Fact-Checking the 1619 Project and Its Critics

1. "We Respond to the Historians Who Critiqued The 1619 Project." 2019. *The New York Times Magazine*, December 20.

2. Transcription: Dunmore's Proclamation. 1775. *Library of Virginia*, November 7.

3. Magness, Phillip W. 2015. "Hamilton & Slavery, Part II." *Phillip W. Magness*, July 10. http://philmagness.com/?p=1330

4. Pocock, Nigel, and Victoria Cook. 2011. "The Business of Enslavement." British Broadcasting Corporation, February 17.

5. The Islands of the Bahamas. 2020. "Queen's Staircase." *The Islands of the Bahamas*.

6. Documents of Parliament (UK). 1788. "Reports of the Lords of the Committee of Council appointed for the consideration of all matters relating to Trade and Foreign Plantations," February 11.

7. "Historical Document: The Quock Walker Case: 'Instructions to the Jury.'" 1783. Public Broadcasting Service. https://www.pbs.org/wgbh/aia/part2/2h38.html

8. "The Northwest Ordinance." 1787. National Archives, Records of the Continental and Confederation Congresses and the Constitutional Convention, 1774–1789: Miscellaneous Papers (Microfilm Publication M332, roll 9, Record Group 360). Passed July 13, 1787.

9. McPherson, James M. 1982. *Ordeal by Fire: The Civil War and Reconstruction*. New York: Alfred Knopf.

10. See McPherson, *Ordeal by Fire*; Magness, Phillip W., and Sebastian N. Page. 2011. *Colonization After Emancipation: Lincoln and the Movement for Black Resettlement*. Columbia: University of Missouri Press.

11. Wilentz, Sean. 2009. "Who Lincoln Was." *The New Republic*, July 15.

12. Gates, Henry Louis Jr. 2009. *Lincoln on Race and Slavery*. Princeton, NJ: Princeton University Press.

13. I was one of the principal co-discoverers of the new materials, including several large caches of diplomatic records from Lincoln's efforts to secure sites for freedmen's colonies in the West Indies that are now housed in Great Britain, Belize, the Netherlands, and Jamaica. 2011. "Lincoln Urged Free Blacks to Resettle Abroad." *CBS News*, March 4. https://www.cbsnews.com/news/lincoln-urged-free-blacks-to-resettle-abroad/

14. Magness, Phillip W. 2015. "The American System and the Political Economy of Black Colonization." *Journal of the History of Economic Thought*, 37(2): 187–202; Magness, Phillip W. 2012. "Wither Liberia? Civil War Emancipation and Freedmen Resettlement

148 | Notes

in West Africa." *The Civil War Monitor*, November 11; Magness, Phillip W. 2013. "The Île à Vache: From Hope to Disaster." *The New York Times*, Opinion Pages, April 12; Page, Sebastian N. 2011. "Lincoln and Chiriquí Colonization Revisited." *American Nineteenth Century History*, 12(3): 289–325.

15. Page, Sebastian. 2012. "Lincoln, Colonization and the Sound of Silence." *The New York Times*, Opinion Pages, December 4; Magness and Page, *Colonization After Emancipation*; Douma, Michael J. 2019. *The Colonization of Freed African Americans in Suriname: Archival Sources Relating to the U.S. Dutch Negotiations, 1860–1866*. Leiden University Press; Douma, Michael J. 2015. "The Lincoln Administration's Negotiations to Colonize African Americans in Dutch Suriname." *Civil War History*, 61(2): 111–137; Magness, Phillip W. 2012. "The British Honduras Colony: Black Emigrationist Support for Colonization in the Lincoln Presidency." *Slavery & Abolition*, 34(1): 39–69.

16. Magness, Phillip W. 2015. "Lincoln and the Case for Ben Butler's Colonization Story." *Phillip W. Magness*, April 16. http://philmagness.com/?p=1213; Magness, Phillip W. 2011. "James Mitchell and the Mystery of the Emigration Office Papers." *Journal of the Abraham Lincoln Association*, 32(2): 50–62.

17. See Magness, Phillip W. 2016. "Abraham Lincoln and Colonization." *Essential Civil War Curriculum*, 1–17. February.

18. Desmond, Matthew. 2019. "American Capitalism Is Brutal. You Can Trace That to the Plantation." *The New York Times*, August 14.

19. Magness, Phillip W. 2019. "How the 1619 Project Rehabilitates the 'King Cotton' Thesis." *National Review*, August 26; Clegg, John J. 2015. "Capitalism and Slavery." *Critical Historical Studies*, 2(2): 281–304; McCloskey, Deirdre N. 2018. "Slavery Did Not Make America Rich." *Reason*, August/September.

20. Magness, Phillip W. 2019. "The Statistical Errors of the Reparations Agenda." American Institute for Economic Research, June 23; Olmstead, Alan L., and Paul W. Rhode. 2018. "Cotton, Slavery, and the New History of Capitalism." *Explorations in Economic History*, January; see chapter herein entitled "The New History of Capitalism Has a 'Whiteness' Problem"; Clegg, John J. 2019. "How Slavery Shaped American Capitalism." *Jacobin*, August 28.

21. Hannah-Jones, Nikole. 2019. "Economists dispute a few of Baptist's calculations but not the book itself nor its thesis." Twitter, August 18. https://twitter.com/nhannah-jones/status/1163030801778401281

22. Miles, Tiya. 2019. "Chained Migration: How Slavery Made Its Way West," "How Slavery Made Wall Street," and "The Enslaved Pecan Pioneer." In "The 1619 Project," *The New York Times Magazine*, August 14.

23. Desmond, Matthew. 2020. "Matthew Desmond Publications." https://scholar.princeton.edu/matthewdesmond/publications-0

6. The Case for Retracting Matthew Desmond's 1619 Project Essay

1. Desmond, Matthew. 2019. "American Capitalism Is Brutal. You Can Trace That to the Plantation." *The New York Times*, August 14.

2. Hannah-Jones, Nikole. 2019. "America Wasn't a Democracy Until Black Americans Made It One." *New York Times*, August 14; Young, Cathy. 2020. "The Fight Over the 1619 Project." *The Bulwark*, February 9.

3. Gleeson-White, Jane. 2012. *Double Entry: How the Merchants of Venice Created Modern Finance*. New York: W. W. Norton & Company.

4. Brazell, David W., Lowell Dworin, and Michael Walsh. 1989. "A History of Federal Tax Depreciation Policy." *U.S. Treasury Department*, Office of Tax Analysis Paper 64.

5. Kantorovich, L. V. 1939. *Mathematical Methods of Organizing and Planning Production*; Nobel Media AB. 2020. "The Sveriges Riksbank Prize in Economic Sciences in Memory of Alfred Nobel 1973." *The Nobel Prize*; Mises, Ludwig von. 1981. *Socialism: An Economic and Sociological Analysis*. Indianapolis: Liberty Fund. Translated by J. Kahane.

6. Rosenthal, Caitlin. 2018. *Accounting for Slavery*, xii. Cambridge, MA: Harvard University Press.

7. Fitzhugh, George. 1854. *Sociology for the South, or The Failure of Free Society* (electronic ed.). Richmond, VA: A. Morris, Publisher.

8. Speech of James Henry Hammond. 1858. "On the Admission of Kansas, Under the Lecompton Constitution" (also known as the "Cotton Is King" speech). *American Antiquarian Society*.

9. Eicholz, Hans. 2019. "Slavery Gave Us Double-Entry Bookkeeping?" *Law and Liberty*, October 2.

10. Olmstead, Alan L., and Paul W. Rhode. 2008. "Biological Innovation and Productivity Growth in the Antebellum Cotton Economy." *Working Paper 14142*, June.

11. Hansen, Bradley A. 2018. "Stop Telling Kanye to Read Ed Baptist." *Bradley A. Hansen's Blog*, May 3; Hansen, Bradley A. 2019. "A Description of the Problems with Edward Baptist's 'The Half Has Never Been Told' for Non-Economists." *Bradley A. Hansen's Blog*, September 2.

12. Conrad, Afred H., and John R. Meyer. 1958. "The Economics of Slavery in the Antebellum South." *Journal of Political Economy*, 66(2): 95–130.

13. Hummel, Jeffrey. 2012. "Deadweight Loss and the American Civil War: The Political Economy of Slavery, Secession, and Emancipation." October 1; Belotta, Tony. "Robert Fogel and Stanley Engerman's Time on the Cross: The Economics of American Negro Slavery (1974) with Phillip W. Magness." *The Age of Jackson Podcast*, episode 90, January 2017; Engerman, Stanley L. 2017. "Review of 'The Business of Slavery and the Rise of American Capitalism, 1815–1860' by Calvin Schermerhorn and 'The Half Has Never Been Told: Slavery and the Making of American Capitalism' by Edward E. Baptist." *Journal of Economic Literature*, 55(2): 637–643.

14. Olmstead, Alan L., and Paul W. Rhode. 2018. "Cotton, Slavery, and the New History of Capitalism." *Explorations in Economic History*, January.

15. Jan, Tracy. 2016. "There's a Bitter New Battle over Whether Slave Torture Was the Foundation of the American Economy." *The Washington Post*, December 12.

16. Hannah-Jones, Nikole. 2019. "Economists dispute a few of Baptist's calculations but not the book itself nor its thesis." Twitter, August 18. https://twitter.com/nhannah-jones/status/1163030801778401281

150 | Notes

17. Murray, J., A. Olmstead, T. Logan, J. Pritchett, and P. Rousseau. 2015. "Roundtable of Reviews for 'The Half Has Never Been Told: Slavery and the Making of American Capitalism' by Edward E. Baptist." *The Journal of Economic History*, 75(3): 919–931.

7. A Comment on the "New" History of American Capitalism

1. Hayek, Friedrich A. 1954. *Capitalism and the Historians*, 9–10. Chicago: University of Chicago Press.

2. For recent examples of inequality research that received both praise by historians and attention for their prescriptive calls for redistributive taxation, see Saez, Emmanuel, and Gabriel Zucman. 2014. "Exploding Wealth Inequality in the United States." Washington Center for Equitable Growth, October 20; Piketty, Thomas. 2014. *Capital in the 21st Century*. Cambridge, MA: Harvard University Press.

3. Schuessler, Jennifer. 2013. "In History Departments, It's Up with Capitalism." *New York Times*, April 6; Adelman, Jeremy, and Jonathan Levy. 2014. "The Fall and Rise of Economic History." *Chronicle of Higher Education*, December 1.

4. See in particular North, Douglass C., and Robert Paul Thomas. 1973. *The Rise of the Western World: A New Economic History*. New York: Cambridge University Press; Mokyr, Joel. 2002. *The Gifts of Athena: Historical Origins of the Knowledge Economy*. Princeton, NJ: Princeton University Press; Mokyr, Joel. 2009. *The Enlightened Economy: An Economic History of Britain 1700–1850*. New Haven, CT: Yale University Press; McCloskey, Deirdre N. 2006. *Bourgeois Virtue*. Hoboken, NJ: John Wiley & Sons; McCloskey, Deirdre N. 2010. *Bourgeois Dignity: Why Economics Can't Explain the Modern World*. Chicago: University of Chicago Press.

5. An interesting assessment of the opinions of economic historians on slavery and a number of other issues may be found in Whaples, Robert. 1995. "Where Is There Consensus Among American Economic Historians? The Results of a Survey on Forty Propositions." *The Journal of Economic History*, 55(1): 139–154. For a review of the literature on slavery, profitability, and the divisions between historians and economists, see Hummel, Jeffrey Rogers. 2012. Chapter 1. In *Deadweight Loss and the American Civil War: The Political Economy of Slavery, Secession, and Emancipation*. October 1.

6. Several abolitionist works advanced this notion as a critique of slavery on the eve of the Civil War. See Atkinson, Edward. 1861. *Cheap Cotton by Free Labor*. Boston: A. Williams & Co.; Olmsted, Frederick Law, and Arthur Meier Schlesinger. 1996. *The Cotton Kingdom: A Traveller's Observations on Cotton and Slavery in the American Slave States: Based Upon Three Former Volumes of Journeys and Investigations by the Same Author*. Boston: Da Capo Press.

7. Conrad, Alfred H., and John R. Meyer. 1958. "The Economics of Slavery in the Ante Bellum South." *The Journal of Political Economy*, 66(2): 95–130; North, Douglas. 1965. "The State of Economic History." *American Economic Review*, 55(1–2): 86–91; Fogel, Robert William, and Stanley L. Engerman. 1995. *Time on the Cross: The Economics of American Negro Slavery*, vol. 1. W. W. Norton & Company. See also Hummel, Introduction and Chapter 1, *Deadweight Loss*.

8. Hummel, Introduction, *Deadweight Loss*.

9. See in particular Johnson, Walter. 2013. *River of Dark Dreams*. Cambridge, MA: Harvard University Press; Baptist, Edward E. 2014. *The Half Has Never Been Told: Slavery and the Making of American Capitalism*. New York: Basic Books; Beckert, Sven. 2015. *Empire of Cotton: A Global History*. New York: Vintage; Schermerhorn, Calvin. 2015. *The Business of Slavery and the Rise of American Capitalism, 1815–1860*. New Haven, CT: Yale University Press; Beckert, Sven, and Seth Rockman. 2016. *Slavery's Capitalism: A New History of American Economic Development*. Philadelphia: University of Pennsylvania Press.

10. Whaples, "Where Is There Consensus Among American Economic Historians?"

11. Christy, David. 1856. Chapter V. In *Cotton Is King: Or, the Culture of Cotton, and Its Relation to Agriculture, Manufactures and Commerce; and Also to the Free Colored People; and to Those who Hold that Slavery Is in Itself Sinful*. New York: Derby & Jackson.

12. Beckert, *Empire of Cotton,* 52; Baptist, *The Half Has Never Been Told,* 321–322.

13. Speech of James H. Hammond. 1858. *Congressional Globe.* 35th Congress (1st Session, March 4): Appendix, p. 70. If the plantation system was as intractable from the global economy as the NHC literature claims, then the Confederacy's diplomatic strategy might have assured rapid intervention in the American Civil War from the European beneficiaries of its yield. As it happened, the strategy was largely a failure. Owsley, F. L. 1959. *King Cotton Diplomacy.* Tuscaloosa, AL: University of Alabama Press.

14. See in particular Parry, Marc. 2016. "Shackles and Dollars." *Chronicle of Higher Education*, December 8; Murray, J., A. Olmstead, T. Logan, J. Pritchett, and P. Rousseau. 2015. "Roundtable of Reviews for 'The Half Has Never Been Told: Slavery and the Making of American Capitalism' by Edward E. Baptist." *The Journal of Economic History*, 75(3): 919–931; Clegg, John J. 2015. "Capitalism and Slavery." *Critical Historical Studies*, 2(2): 281–304; Baptist, Edward E. 2015. "Correcting an Incorrect 'Corrective.'" *The Junto*, November 4; Olmstead, Alan L., and Paul W. Rhode. 2018. "Cotton, Slavery, and the New History of Capitalism." *Explorations in Economic History* 67: 1–17, January.

15. Olmstead and Rhode, "Cotton, Slavery, and the New History of Capitalism"; Hansen, Bradley A. 2014. "The Back of Ed Baptist's Envelope." *Bradley A. Hansen's Blog*, October 30. http://bradleyahansen.blogspot.com/2014/10/the-back-of-ed-baptists-envelope.html

16. Friedman, Milton, and Anna Jacobson Schwartz. 2008. *A Monetary History of the United States, 1867–1960*. Princeton, NJ: Princeton University Press; Cole, Harold L., and Lee E. Ohanian. 2004. "New Deal Policies and the Persistence of the Great Depression: A General Equilibrium Analysis." *Journal of Political Economy* 112(4): 779–716; Higgs, Robert. 2006. Chapter 1. In *Depression, War, and Cold War: Studies in Political Economy*. Oxford: Oxford University Press.

17. Greif, Avner. 1997. "Cliometrics After 40 Years." *The American Economic Review*, 87(2): 400–403.

18. Rockman, Seth. 2014. "What Makes the History of Capitalism Newsworthy?" *Journal of the Early Republic*, 34(3): 442.

19. Beckert, Sven, Angus Burgin, Peter James Hudson, Louis Hyman, Naomi Lamoreaus, Scott Marler, Stephen Mihm, Julia Ott, Philip Scranton, and Elizabeth Tandy Shermer. 2014. "Interchange: The History of Capitalism." *Journal of American History*, 101(2): 503–536.

152 | *Notes*

20. Cutterham, Tom. 2014. "Is the History of Capitalism the History of Everything?" *The Junto*, September 2.

21. Rockman, "What Makes the History of Capitalism Newsworthy?," 444.

22. Beckert, *Empire of Cotton*, 37.

23. Beckert, Sven. 2014. "Slavery and Capitalism." *Chronicle of Higher Education*, December 12.

24. Beckert, *Empire of Cotton*, xvi.

25. See in particular, Smith, Adam. 1776. Book III, Chapter II and Book IV, Chapter VIII. In *An Inquiry into the Nature and Causes of the Wealth of Nations*.

26. Johnson, *River of Dark Dreams*, 14.

27. Becker, Gary S. 1957. *The Economics of Discrimination*. Chicago: University of Chicago Press; Hutt, William H. 1964. *Economics of the Colour Bar*. London: Institute of Economic Affairs.

28. Smith, Adam. *Lectures on Jurisprudence*. Available in *The Glasgow Edition of the Works and Correspondence of Adam Smith*, 181. 1982. Indianapolis: Liberty Fund.

29. Beckert, *Empire of Cotton*, 37.

30. Atkinson, *Cheap Cotton by Free Labor*; Cairnes, John E. 1862. *The Slave Power: Its Character, Career, and Probable Designs*. New York.

31. Carlyle, Thomas. 1849. "Occassional Discourse on the Negro Question." *Fraser's Magazine for Town and Country*, February. See also Levy, David M. 2002. *How the Dismal Science Got Its Name: Classical Economics and the Ur-Text of Racial Politics*. Ann Arbor: University of Michigan Press.

32. Carlyle, Thomas. 1850. *Latter Day Pamphlets*, 34. London: Chapman & Hall.

33. Carlyle, Thomas. 1867. *Shooting Niagara: And After?* London: Chapman & Hall.

34. Fitzhugh, George. 1857. *Cannibals All! Or, Slaves Without Masters* (electronic ed.), 79. Richmond, VA: A. Morris, Publisher. https://docsouth.unc.edu/southlit/fitzhughcan/fitzcan.html

35. Fitzhugh, George. 1854. *Sociology for the South, or The Failure of Free Society* (electronic ed.), 7, 10, 188. Richmond, VA: A. Morris, Publisher. https://docsouth.unc.edu/southlit/fitzhughsoc/fitzhugh.html

36. Beckert, *Empire of Cotton*, xv, 78.

37. Leonard, Thomas C. 2009. "Origins of the Myth of Social Darwinism: The Ambiguous Legacy of Richard Hofstadter's Social Darwinism in American Thought." *Journal of Economic Behavior & Organization*, 71(1): 37–51; Zwolinski, Matt. 2015. "Social Darwinism and Social Justice: Herbert Spencer on Our Duties to the Poor." In *Distributive Justice Debates in Social and Political Thought: Perspectives on Finding a Fair Share*, ed. Camilla Boisen and Matthew Murray. New York: Routledge Publishing.

38. For a related history of both Hamilton's transmission to the German Historical School and its continued influence upon the historical profession, see Eicholz, Hans L. 2014. "Hamilton, Harvard, and the German Historical School: A Short Note on a Curious History." *Journal of Private Enterprise*, 29(3): 43.

39. Recent examples include Mehrotra, Ajay K. 2013. *Making the Modern American Fiscal State: Law, Politics, and the Rise of Progressive Taxation, 1877–1929*. Cambridge: Cambridge University Press; Fink, Leon. 2014. *The Long Gilded Age: American Capitalism and the Lessons of a New World Order*. Philadelphia: University of Pennsylvania Press.

40. Leonard, Thomas C. 2003. "'More Merciful and Not Less Effective': Eugenics and American Economics in the Progressive Era." *History of Political Economy* 35(4): 687–712; Leonard, Thomas C. 2016. *Illiberal Reformers: Race, Eugenics, and American Economics in the Progressive Era*. Princeton, NJ: Princeton University Press.

41. Keynes, John Maynard. 1923. "Is Britain Overpopulated?" *New Republic*, October 31; Keynes, John Maynard. 2010. "The End of Laissez-Faire." *Essays in Persuasion*, 272–294. London: Palgrave Macmillan; Magness, Phillip W., and Hernandez, Sean J. 2017. "The Economic Eugenicism of John Maynard Keynes." *Journal of Markets and Morality*, 20(1): 79–100.

42. Hofstadter, Richard. 1944. *Social Darwinism in American Thought*. Boston: Beacon Press. For a critique of Hofstadter, arguing that he overstated and misinterpreted his evidence, see Zwolinski, "Social Darwinism and Social Justice."

43. Mises, Ludwig von. 1927. "Das Ende des Laissez-Faire, Ideen zur Verbindung von Privat und Gemeinwirtschaft." *Zeitschrift für die gesamte Staatswissenschaft* 82: 190–91. Translation by Joseph Stromberg, available at https://mises.org/library/mises-keynes-1927

8. The New History of Capitalism Has a "Whiteness" Problem

1. Hannah-Jones, Nikole, ed. "The 1619 Project." *The New York Times.*

2. Mackaman, Tom. 2019. "An Interview with Historian James McPherson on the New York Times' 1619 Project." *World Socialist Web Site*, November 14, https://www.wsws.org/en/articles/2019/11/14/mcph-n14.html; Mackaman, Tom. 2019. "An Interview with Historian Gordon Wood on the New York Times' 1619 Project." *World Socialist Web Site*, November 28. https://www.wsws.org/en/articles/2019/11/28/wood-n28.html; Mackaman, Tom. 2019. "An Interview with Historian James Oakes on the New York Times' 1619 Project." *World Socialist Web Site*, November 18. https://www.wsws.org/en/articles/2019/11/18/oake-n18.html

3. Magness, Phillip W. 2019. "How the 1619 Project Rehabilitates the 'King Cotton' Thesis." *National Review*, August 26.

4. McPherson, James M. 2015. "Lincoln's Civil War Brilliance: The Real Story of the Political Savvy That Helped End Slavery." *Salon*, March 28.

5. Magness, Phillip W., and Sebastian N. Page. 2011. *Colonization After Emancipation: Lincoln and the Movement for Black Resettlement*. Columbia: University of Missouri Press.

6. Rockman, Seth. 2019. "Honestly, do the socialists think GW is down with their project?" Twitter, November 28. https://twitter.com/sethrockman/status/1200148036208361472

7. Park, Benjamin. 2019. "Remember when McPherson couldn't name a single non-white or non-male academic historian?" Twitter, November 28. https://twitter.com/BenjaminEPark/status/1200261304793083904

8. Magness, Phillip W. 2019. "How Twitter Is Corrupting the History Profession." American Institute for Economic Research, August 29.

9. Desmond, Matthew. 2019. "American Capitalism Is Brutal. You Can Trace That to the Plantation." *The New York Times*, August 14.

154 | *Notes*

10. Magness, Phillip W. 2019. "A Comment on the 'New' History of American Capitalism." American Institute for Economic Research, August 17.

11. Engerman, Stanley L. 2017. "Review of 'The Business of Slavery and the Rise of American Capitalism, 1815–1860' by Calvin Schermerhorn and 'The Half Has Never Been Told: Slavery and the Making of American Capitalism' by Edward E. Baptist." *Journal of Economic Literature*, 55(2): 637–643.

12. Olmstead, Alan L., and Paul W. Rhode. 2018. "Cotton, Slavery, and the New History of Capitalism." *Explorations in Economic History*, January.

13. See chapter herein entitled "The Statistical Errors of the Reparations Agenda."

14. Sutch, Richard C. 2018. "The Economics of African American Slavery: The Cliometrics Debate." NBER Working Paper no. 25197, October.

15. Davis, David Brion. 1988. "The Benefit of Slavery." *The New York Review of Books*, March 31.

16. Neptune, H. Reuben. 2019. "Throwin' Scholarly Shade: Eric Williams in the New Histories of Capitalism and Slaver." *Journal of the Early Republic*, 39(2): 299–326.

9. What the 1619 Project's Critics Get Wrong About Lincoln

1. See chapter herein entitled "The Case for Retracting Matthew Desmond's 1619 Project Essay."

2. Guelzo, Allen C. 2020. "The 1619 Project's Outrageous, Lying Slander of Abe Lincoln." *New York Post*, March 3; Wilentz, Sean. 2020. "A Matter of Facts." *The Atlantic*, January 22.

3. Wilentz, "A Matter of Facts"; Lincoln, Abraham. 1862. The first edition of Abraham Lincoln's preliminary emancipation proclamation, September 22. Available from *The Alfred Whital Stern Collection of Lincolniana*.

4. "Transcription: An Act for the Release of Certain Persons Held to Service or Labor in the District of Columbia." National Archives. https://www.archives.gov/exhibits/featured-documents/dc-emancipation-act/transcription.html

5. Magness, Phillip W. n.d. "Lincoln to Crummell, 5/5/1862." *Phillip W. Magness*. http://philmagness.com/?page_id=407

6. Magness, Phillip W. 2014. "A Brief Guide to Colonization Documents Omitted from the Collected Works of Abraham Lincoln." *Phillip W. Magness*, January 7. http://philmagness.com/?p=648

7. Magness, Phillip W., and Sebastian N. Page. 2011. *Colonization After Emancipation: Lincoln and the Movement for Black Resettlement.* Columbia: University of Missouri Press.

8. Scheips, Paul J. 1952. "Lincoln and the Chiriqui Colonization Project." *The Journal of Negro History*, 37(4): 418–453; Lincoln, Abraham. 1862. "Annual Message to Congress." In *Collected Works of Abraham Lincoln*, vol. 5: 519–537.

9. Page, Sebastian N. 2017. "'A Knife Sharp Enough to Divide Us': William H. Seward, Abraham Lincoln, and Black Colonization." *Diplomatic History*, 41(2): 362–391.

10. Douma, Michael J. 2019. *The Colonization of Freed African Americans in Suriname: Archival Sources Relating to the U.S.-Dutch Negotiations, 1860–1866.* Leiden, Netherlands: Leiden University Press.

Notes | 155

11. Page, Sebastian N. 2011. "Lincoln and Chiriqui Colonization Revisited." *American Nineteenth Century History*, 12(3): 289–325.

12. Magness, Phillip W. n.d. "Thaddeus Stevens and Colonization." *Phillip W. Magness*. http://philmagness.com/?page_id=470

13. "Twelve Scholars Critique the 1619 Project and the New York Times Magazine Editor Responds." 2020. *History News Network*, January 26.

10. The 1619 Project: An Epitaph

1. Silverstein, Jake. 2020. "An Update to The 1619 Project." *The New York Times*, March 11.

2. Silverstein, Jake. 2019. "We Respond to the Historians Who Critiqued The 1619 Project." *The New York Times*, December 20.

3. See chapter herein entitled "Fact-Checking the 1619 Project and Its Critics."

4. See chapter herein entitled "How the 1619 Project Rehabilitates the 'King Cotton' Thesis."

5. See chapter herein entitled "The Case for Retracting Matthew Desmond's 1619 Project Essay."

6. Young, Cathy. 2020. "The Fight Over the 1619 Project." *The Bulwark*, February 9.

7. Hannah-Jones, Nikole. 2019. "And this dude is defending that shit, actually arguing we should take this 'preeminent' scholar seriously." Twitter, November 22. https://twitter.com/nhannahjones/status/1197762958039932928; Hannah-Jones, Nikole. 2019. "Who considers him preeminent? I don't." Twitter, November 22. https://twitter.com/nhannahjones/status/1197764022550122496

8. Hannah-Jones, Nikole. 2019. "LOL. Right, because white historians have produced truly objective history." Twitter, November 21. https://twitter.com/nhannahjones/status/1197573220037201922; see chapter herein entitled "The New History of Capitalism Has a 'Whiteness' Problem."

9. 1776 Unites. 2020. "1776 Project"; Rosen, Christine. 2020. "The 'Beyonce of Journalism' and Her Critics." *Commentary*, February 18; Hemingway, Mark. 2020. "The New York Times Goes All In on Flawed 1619 Project." *RealClearPolitics*, February 21.

10. See chapter herein entitled "The Statistical Errors of the Reparations Agenda."

11. Murray, J., A. Olmstead, T. Logan, J. Pritchett, and P. Rousseau. 2015. "Roundtable of Reviews for 'The Half Has Never Been Told: Slavery and the Making of American Capitalism' by Edward E. Baptist." *The Journal of Economic History*, 75(3): 919–931.

12. Harris, Leslie M. 2020. "I Helped Fact-Check the 1619 Project. The Times Ignored Me." *Politico*, March 6.

11. Should K–12 Classrooms Teach from the 1619 Project?

1. Schulte, Mark, Fareed Mostoufi, and Hannah Berk. 2019. "*The 1619 Project*: Pulitzer Center Education Programming." https://pulitzercenter.org/projects/1619-project-pulitzer-center-education-programming

2. Hannah-Jones, Nikole. Twitter, https://x.com/nhannahjones/status/1163541978954510337 (now deleted).

156 | *Notes*

3. Krugman, Paul, and Robin Wells. 2024. *Economics*, 7th ed. New York: Macmillan Learning.

4. Terry Gross. 2020. "A Call for Reparations: How America Might Narrow the Racial Wealth Gap." *Fresh Air*, June 20. https://www.npr.org/transcripts/882773218

5. Silverstein, Jake. 2020. "An Update to the 1619 Project." *The New York Times*, March 11.

6. Hannah-Jones, Nikole. Twitter, https://x.com/nhannahjones/status/1274389358758506497 (now deleted).

7. Harris, Leslie M. 2020. "I Helped Fact-Check the 1619 Project. The Times Ignored Me." *Politico*, March 6.

8. Olmstead, Alan, and Paul W. Rhode. 2018. "Cotton, Slavery, and the New History of Capitalism." *Explorations in Economic History*, 67: 1–17; Wright, Gavin. 2020. "Slavery and Anglo-American Capitalism Revisited." *The Economic History Review*, 73(2): 353–383.

12. Down the 1619 Project's Memory Hole

1. Stephens, Bret. 2020. "The 1619 Chronicles." *The New York Times*, October 9.

2. Goldberg, Jonah. 2020. "The New York Times Should Explain Its Stealth Edits to the 1619 Project." American Enterprise Institute, September 25. https://www.aei.org/op-eds/the-nyt-should-explain-its-stealth-edits-to-the-1619-project/

3. Friedersdorf, Conor (@conor64). 2020. "This claim is staggering …" (thread). Twitter, September 18 (since deleted; screenshot is available at https://archive.is/pwP48).

4. Friedersdorf, "This claim is staggering …"

5. Magness, Philip W. 2020. "The Case for Retracting Matthew Desmond's 1619 Project Essay." American Institute for Economic Research, February 11 (archived at https://archive.is/o6bVW).

6. Harris, Leslie M. 2020. "I Helped Fact-Check the 1619 Project. The Times Ignored Me." *Politico*, March 6 (archived at https://archive.is/JIsPu).

7. Friedersdorf, Conor. 2020. "1776 Honors America's Diversity in a Way 1619 Does Not." *The Atlantic*, January 6 (archived at https://archive.is/qaB3J).

8. CNN (@CNN). 2020. "The 1619 Project 'does not argue …'" Twitter, September 18, 11:52 a.m. (archived at https://archive.is/RfuvS).

9. Ida Bae Wells (@nhannahjones). 2020. "One thing in which the right has been tremendously successful …" Twitter, September 18, 6:03 a.m. (screenshot archived at https://archive.is/DRBwA).

10. Friedersdorf, "This claim is staggering …"

11. Konopka, Rafal (@rafalkonopka). 2020. "This is the print cover of the 1619 project issue …" Twitter, September 18, 7:54 p.m. https://x.com/rafalkonopka/status/1307105863375687682

12. "The 1619 Project." 2019. *The New York Times*, August 18 (pdf available at the Pulitzer Center website: https://pulitzercenter.org/sites/default/files/full_issue_of_the_1619_project.pdf).

13. "The 1619 Project." 2024. *The New York Times* (archived at https://archive.is/nNAhu).

13. The Suicide of the American Historical Association

1. "Message from James H. Sweet." 2022. American Historical Association, August 19. https://www.historians.org/news/message-from-james-h-sweet/

2. Sweet, James H. 2022. "Is History History?" Historians.org, August 17. https://www.historians.org/perspectives-article/is-history-history-identity-politics-and-teleologies-of-the-present-september-2022/

3. Denial, Cate (@cjdenial). 2022. "If, like me, you're appalled by James Sweet's essay …" (thread). Twitter, August 17, 9:04 p.m. https://x.com/cjdenial/status/1560070136010268672

4. American Historical Association (@AHAhistorians). 2022. "How do historians undertake their chosen profession …," Twitter, August 17, 1:18 p.m. (quotes, https://x.com/AHAhistorians/status/1559952700795666432/quotes).

5. b-boy bouiebaisse (@jbouie). 2022. "Bold take from [checks byline] the president of AHA …" Twitter, August 17, 6:41 p.m. https://x.com/jbouie/status/1560034087749943303

6. Potter, Claire (@TenuredRadical). 2022. "P.S. I can't help but think that Sweet has not read the 1619 Project …" Twitter, August 17, 8:46 p.m. https://x.com/TenuredRadical/status/1560065500981362689

7. Magness, Phillip W. 2020. "Should K–12 Classrooms Teach from the 1619 Project?" American Institute for Economic Research, September 12. https://www.aier.org/article/should-k-12-classrooms-teach-from-the-1619-project/

8. Magness, Phillip W. "The Case for Retracting Matthew Desmond's 1619 Project Essay." American Institute for Economic Research, February 11. https://www.aier.org/article/the-case-for-retracting-matthew-desmonds-1619-project-essay/

9. Walsh, David Austin (@DavidAstinWalsh). 2022. "One of my early critiques of the anti-1619 literature …" Twitter, August 20, 8:59 a.m. https://x.com/DavidAstinWalsh/status/1560974922045968390

10. Murdock, Corinne. 2020. "UVA Fellow, George Mason Professor: Overthrow the Government If Trump Wins." *Tennessee Star*, November 3. https://tennesseestar.com/news/uva-fellow-former-george-mason-professor-overthrow-the-government-if-trump-wins/cmurdock/2020/11/03/

11. American Historical Association (@AHAhistorians). 2022. "Please read this apology from James H. Sweet …" Twitter, August 19, 5:16 p.m. https://x.com/AHAhistorians/status/1560737391958433792

12. Gannon, Kevin (@TheTattooedProf). 2022. "Summing up: the President of my professional organization …" Twitter, August 20, 11:51 a.m. https://x.com/TheTattooedProf/status/1561018161465593856

13. (((it's DOCTOR, not Ms.))) (@NotOccupying). 2022. "This is why I don't think Sweet's 'apology' was sincere …" Twitter, August 20, 10:41 a.m. https://x.com/NotOccupying/status/1561000479450189826

14. Gannon, Kevin. 2022. "On Presentism and History; or, We're Doing This Again, Are We?" *TheTattooedProf*, August 19. https://thetattooedprof.com/2022/08/19/on-presentism-and-history-or-were-doing-this-again-are-we/

15. Burnett, L. D. (@LDBurnett). Twitter. August 20, 2022. https://x.com/LDBurnett/status/1560971258358927360 (now deleted).

16. Burnett, L. D. (@LDBurnett). Twitter. August 20, 2022. https://x.com/LDBurnett/status/1560972870485827585 (now deleted).

17. Magness, Phillip W. 2019. "How Twitter Is Corrupting the History Profession." American Institute for Economic Research, August 29. https://www.aier.org/article/how-twitter-is-corrupting-the-history-profession/

14. The 1619 Project Unrepentantly Pushes Junk History

1. Magness, Phillip W. 2013. "The Île à Vache: From Hope to Disaster." *The New York Times Disunion Blog*, April 12.

2. Zora Neale Hurston. 1942. *Dust Tracks on a Road*, 284. New York: J. B. Lippincott.

3. Hurston, *Dust Tracks on a Road*.

4. Board of Governors of the Federal Reserve System. 2024. "Distribution of Household Wealth in the U.S. Since 1989." https://www.federalreserve.gov/releases/z1/dataviz/dfa/distribute/chart/#range:1989.3,2021.3;quarter:128;series:Net%20worth;demographic:networth;population:1;units:shares

5. Olmstead, A. L., and P. W. Rhode. 2010. "Productivity Growth and the Regional Dynamics of Antebellum Southern Development." National Bureau of Economic Research Working Paper No. 16494.

6. Olmstead, A. L., and P. W. Rhode. 2018. "Cotton, Slavery, and the New History of Capitalism." *Explorations in Economic History*, 67, 1–17.

7. Franklin, Benjamin. 1904 (1768–1772). *The Works of Benjamin Franklin, Including the Private as well as the Official and Scientific Correspondence, Together with the Unmutilated and Correct Version of the Autobiography*, vol. 5, ed. John Bigelow. New York: G. P. Putnam's Sons. https://oll.libertyfund.org/titles/bigelow-the-works-of-benjamin-franklin-vol-v-letters-and-misc-writings-1768-1772

8. Mares, I., and D. Queralt. 2015. "The Non-democratic Origins of Income Taxation." *Comparative Political Studies*, 48(14): 1974–2009.

9. Sombart, Werner. 1906. *Why Is There No Socialism in the United States?* Tübingen, Germany: Verlag von J. C. B. Mohr.

10. Hurston, *Dust Tracks on a Road*, 286.

15. Hulu's *1619* Docuseries Peddles False History

1. Goldberg, Jonah. 2020. "New York Times Discredits Itself by Going Along with Rewriting Facts of 1619 Project." *New York Post*, September 27. https://nypost.com/2020/09/27/nyt-discredits-itself-by-rewriting-the-facts-of-the-1619-project/

2. Holton, W. 2021. *Liberty Is Sweet: The Hidden History of the American Revolution*. New York: Simon & Schuster.

3. Davis, Jefferson. 1865. General Orders No. 14, March 23. In *The War of the Rebellion: A Compilation of the Official Records of the Union and Confederate Armies*, series IV, vol. III, p. 1161. Washington, DC: Government Printing Office.

16. The 1619 Project's Confusion on Capitalism

1. Sutch, Richard C. 2018. "The Economics of African American Slavery: The Cliometrics Debate." National Bureau of Economic Research Working Paper No. 25197. http://www.nber.org/papers/w25197

2. Magness, "The Case for Retracting Matthew Desmond's 1619 Project Essay." American Institute for Economic Research, February 11. https://www.aier.org/article/the-case-for-retracting-matthew-desmonds-1619-project-essay/

3. Olmstead, Alan L., and Paul W. Rhode. 2018. "Cotton, Slavery, and the New History of Capitalism." *Explorations in Economic History*, 67 (January): 1–17.

4. Rockman, Seth. 2014. "Review: What Makes the History of Capitalism Newsworthy?" *Journal of the Early Republic*, 34(3): 439–466.

5. Wright, Gavin. 2020. "Slavery and Anglo-American Capitalism Revisited." *The Economic History Review*, 73(2): 353–383.

6. Magness, Phillip W. 2019. "The Statistical Errors of the Reparations Agenda." American Institute for Economic Research, June 23. https://www.aier.org/article/the-statistical-errors-of-the-reparations-agenda/

7. Nunn, Nathan. 2007. "Slavery, Inequality, and Economic Development in the Americas: An Examination of the Engerman-Sokoloff Hypothesis." Department of Economics, Harvard University, and National Bureau of Economic Research. https://scholar.harvard.edu/files/nunn/files/domestic_slavery.pdf

8. Magness, Phillip W. 2019. "How the 1619 Project Rehabilitates the 'King Cotton' Thesis." *National Review*, August 26. https://www.nationalreview.com/2019/08/1619-project-new-york-times-king-cotton-thesis/

9. Conrad, Alfred H., and John R. Meyer. 1958. "The Economics of Slavery in the Ante Bellum South." *The Journal of Political Economy*, 66(2): 95–130.

10. Magness, Phillip W., and Michael Makovi. 2023. "The Mainstreaming of Marx: Measuring the Effect of the Russian Revolution on Karl Marx's Influence." *The Journal of Political Economy*, 131(6): 1507–1545.

11. Palmer, Annie. 2022. "Amazon Workers in Alabama Reject Union for Second Time, but Challenged Ballots Remain." CNBC, March 31. https://www.cnbc.com/2022/03/31/amazon-workers-in-alabama-reject-union-for-second-time.html

12. Moreno, Paul. 2010. "Unions and Discrimination." *Cato Journal*, 30(1): 67–85.

13. Moreno, Paul D. 2006. *Black Americans and Organized Labor: A New History*, 172. Baton Rouge: Louisiana State University Press.

14. Kelley, Robin D. G. 2015. *Hammer and Hoe: Alabama Communists During the Great Depression* (25th anniversary ed.). Chapel Hill: University of North Carolina Press.

15. National Association for the Advancement of Colored People. 1956. *NAACP: An American Organization*. https://www.crmvet.org/docs/5606_naacp_pamphlet.pdf

16. "W. E. B. Du Bois and Mao Tse-Tung, ca. 1959" (photograph). 1959. W. E. B. Du Bois Papers (MS 312), Special Collections and University Archives, University of Massachusetts Amherst Libraries. https://credo.library.umass.edu/view/full/mums312-i0684

17. Du Bois, W. E. B. 1953. "On Stalin." Marxists Internet Archive. https://www.marxists.org/reference/archive/stalin/biographies/1953/03/16.htm

18. Sombart, Werner. 1906. *Why Is There No Socialism in the United States?* Tübingen, Germany: Verlag von J. C. B. Mohr.

19. Grayson, William J. 1907. *Selected Poems by William J. Grayson*, 23. New York: Neale Publishing Company.

20. Oakes, James. 2021. "What the 1619 Project Got Wrong." *Catalyst*, 5(3); Coclanis, Peter A. 2021. "Capitalism, Slavery, and Matthew Desmond's Low-Road Contribution to the 1619 Project." Independent Institute, August 12. https://www.independent.org/publications/article.asp?id=13705

17. The Tooth-Fairy Economics of Slavery Reparations

1. Henderson, David R., and Phillip W. Magness. 2023. "'The 1619 Project' on Hulu Vindicates Capitalism." *Wall Street Journal*, February 20.

2. Darity, William, Jr., A. Kirsten Mullen, and Marvin Slaughter. 2022. "The Cumulative Costs of Racism and the Bill for Black Reparations." *Journal of Economic Perspectives*, 36(2): 99–122.

Index

A

abolitionist movement, 7, 12, 13–18, 26, 56, 70, 122, 128; British, 129–130; and laissez-faire capitalism, 36

Accounting for Slavery (Rosenthal), 37–38, 116

Amazon warehouses, 131, 132–133, 137, 139–140

American Anti-Slavery Society, 13

American Historical Association, 104–109

American Revolution: history of, 33, 34; and slavery, ix, xiii, 24–28, 36, 65, 73, 74, 81–85, 89, 92, 97, 111, 112, 118–121, 125–130

Anderson, Carol, 21–22

anti-capitalism: in the 1619 project, xiii, 116, 135, 139; as historical method, 56–58; and the NHC, xiii, 67; and progressive history, 59–62. *See also* capitalism

anti-monopoly laws, 60

Appomattox Courthouse, 130

Araujo, Ana Lucia, 66

Arthur Tappan & Co., 13–15

Atkinson, Edward, 62

B

Bahamas, 26

Baptist, Ed: conflating slavery with Excel, 116–117; critique of, 68, 69, 117–118; equating capitalism with slavery, 2, 20–22, 40–42, 116–118, 132; misrepresentation by, 2, 3, 4, 5, 9, 19, 20–22, 49, 50, 51, 52, 68, 71; and the NHC, 9, 67

Baradaran, Mehrsa, 33

Barbados, 27

Bastiat, Frederic, 7

Bates, Edward, 78

Beckert, Sven, 2, 38, 49, 54, 55, 56, 58, 67, 71

Before the Mayflower (Bennett), 111

Benezet, Anthony, 120

Bennett, Lerone Jr., 111

Berlin, Ira, 68

Biden, Joseph R., 95, 144

Biden administration, 142

biology, racial, 61

Booth, John Wilkes, 79

Bouie, Jamelle, 90, 106

Bunker Hill, Battle of, 129

Burnett, Lora, 108

Bynum, Victoria, 23

C

Cairnes, J. E., 62

Capital (Marx), 11

capitalism: and the 1619 Project, 131–140; and the abolitionist movement, 36; American, 65, 66, 74, 83; and classical liberalism, 46; and credit, 17; critique of, 2, 5, 7, 8, 9–11, 12, 17, 31, 35, 43–45, 56–62; defects/failures of, 60, 61, 62; definition of, 45–46, 53–54, 62, 132, 133; and emancipation, 70; emotional aversion to, 43; as exploitative, 133, 136; free market, 10, 17, 38, 67, 116; free-labor, 11; history of, 17, 52, 53, 56, 60, 61–63, 134, 139; idealized conception of, 45; as illiberal system, 56; industrial, 48, 70; intellectual history of, 36; laissez-faire, 14, 36, 57, 59, 60, 61, 122; market, 22, 52, 54–55, 56, 57, 134; modern, xiii, 55, 70, 83, 133; pre-progressive era, 59; racial slave, 10, 55, 58, 136, 137; as racist, 9; and slavery, vii, xiii, 2–3, 7, 17–18, 21–22, 24, 31–32, 38–39, 42, 47, 50, 53–58, 60, 62, 65, 68, 70, 71, 99, 115, 117, 122, 133–134; Smithian, 56; theorists of, 56, 59; wage labor, 11; war, 10, 49, 55, 58. *See also* anti-capitalism; free market

Capitalism and Slavery (Williams), 70

162 | *Index*

CARES Act, 143
Caribbean Islands. *See* West Indies
Carleton, Guy, 25
Carlyle, Thomas, 12, 57, 59
Chatham Incident, 13–14
Christy, David, 2
city planning, xi
civil rights, 137
civil rights movement, 138
Civil War, 1, 33, 34, 82, 134
Clarkson, Thomas, 26
Clay, Henry, 55
climate change policies, 10
cliometric scholarship, 47, 50, 51, 52
Clotilda (slave ship), 114
Coates, Ta-Nehisi, 19–20, 21, 22; call for reparations, 3, 19
Cobden, Richard, 7, 62
collectivism, Darwinian, 59
colonialism, 56
colonization, vii, xiii–xiv, 28–31, 66, 72–80, 112–113
Colonization after Emancipation (Magness & Page), 112
commercialism, 57
Commons, John R., 61
communism, 12, 37, 136
Communist Party, 138
Confederacy, 1, 2, 50
Conrad, Alfred, 41, 136
contract law, 46
Cooper, Dan, 17
Cornish, Samuel, 13
cotton: claimed economic importance of, xiii, 1–3, 19, 20, 21, 39, 49–50, 83, 89, 117, 132, 134–135; production of, 3–4; technological improvements, 4, 40, 117–118, 132
credit economy, 15–16
credit-reporting firms, 16–17
Critical Race Theory, 143
critical theory, 68
Crummell, Alexander, 75
Cutterham, Tom, 53

D

Darity, William A., 143, 144
Darwinism, social, 59, 61
Davis, David Brion, 21
Davis, Jefferson, 130
De Bow, J. D. B., 55
Declaration of Independence, 25, 83

Democratic Party, 36, 142
Denial, Cate, 105
depreciation, 37
Desmond, Matthew: "Capitalism" essay, vii, xii–xiii, 2, 7, 24, 31–32, 71, 81, 115, 131, 132, 136–137, 138–139; case for retracting his essay, 35–42; expanded essay, ix, 112; factual errors, ix, 35, 67, 83, 89, 92, 99, 111, 116–118, 121–123, 131; and New History of Capitalism, 43; questionable scholarly expertise, ix, xii, 33, 90, 106, 119, 132
Doolittle, James, 76
double-entry bookkeeping, 37, 39
Douglass, Frederick, 28, 76–77
drug policies, 61
Du Bois, W. E. B., 67, 138
Duke University, 115
Dun & Bradstreet, 16
Dunmore, John Murray (4th earl of), 24, 26, 82, 120–121, 125, 126–129, 130
Dunmore Proclamation, 82, 83, 84, 120–121, 126–127, 128, 129, 130
Dust Tracks on a Road (Hurston), 113, 114

E

economic history, 4, 35, 44, 46, 47–48, 50, 51, 52, 56, 68, 132; American, 3, 66, 135; of slavery, 69, 83
economics: classical, 56; as exploitative, 131; plantation, 132; progressive era, 59–60; of slavery, ix, 5, 32, 33, 47–48, 50, 67, 83, 89, 90, 111, 119, 131
Edge Frederick Milnes, 75
Ely, Richard T., 61
Emancipation Proclamation, 29, 74–75, 76, 120, 127, 130
eminent domain, 142
empiricism, evidentiary, 46, 62
Engerman, Stanley, 4–5, 20–21, 47, 68, 69
English common law, 24
eugenics, 61
exploitation theory, 10, 11, 54, 56, 59, 122, 133, 136

F

Fairfax Resolves, 129
Federal Reserve, 143
feudalism, 133
Fitzhugh, George, 5, 7, 8, 10–11, 12, 38, 55, 57–58, 59, 122
Fogel, Robert, 47, 69
Foulke, Roy A., 17

Fox, Charles James, 26
Franklin, Benjamin, 120
free market, xiii, 3, 5, 7–12, 13, 17, 38, 60, 61, 67, 103, 116, 122, 133. *See also* capitalism
free trade, 7, 14, 58
Freedmen's Bureau, 79
Friedersdorf, Conor, 96
Fugitive Slave Act (1850), 17

G

Gannon, Kevin, 108
Garner, Henry Highland, 77
Garrison, William Lloyd, 14
Gates, Henry Louis Jr., 29
Genovese, Eugene, 68
German Historical School, 59
Gilded Age, 60
Goldin, Claudia, 69
Grayson, William J., 139
Great Depression, 51
Great Enrichment, 45
Green New Deal, 139
Greif, Avner, 51
Grinder, Brian, 17
Guelzo, Allen, 74–75, 76, 78, 79, 80

H

Haiti, 76, 77
Half Has Never Been Told, The (Baptist), 3, 20, 40, 42, 68, 117
Hamilton, Alexander, 25, 60, 121
Hammond, James Henry, 2, 50
Hannah-Jones, Nikole: activist approach to history, x, xi–xii, 118; arguments about American Revolution, xiii, 24, 25, 27–28, 125–130; criticism of, 28–29, 31, 65; dismissal of scholarly critics by, viii, ix, 4, 35, 42, 83–85, 89–90, 103–105, 106, 113, 119; editorial decisions of, viii–ix, ix, 83, 92, 111–112, 114, 118–121, 119; edits to 1619 essay, viii, 81–85, 89, 95, 96, 97, 99–101, 114, 116, 118–121, 126; expanded essay, ix, 112; factual inaccuracies of, vii, 132, 136; in Hulu docuseries, ix–x, 125–129, 131, 132–134; introduction to hardback publication, 115; introductory essay, xi–xii, 123; lacking scholarly guidance, 32–34, 87–88; on Lincoln, 28–29, 30, 66, 73, 74, 77; Pulitzer Prize awarded to, 95, 96; questionable scholarly expertise, 119; on reparations, vii, x, xii, 89, 115, 138, 141–144; strategic edits by, 95–97

Hansen, Bradley, 20
Harlan, James, 78
Harris, Leslie M., viii–ix, 84–85, 92, 99, 111, 119
Hay, John, 75, 78
Hayek, F. A., xiii, 43, 44, 56, 62
Henderson, David R., 141
Henry, Patrick, 129
Hilt, Eric, 4
historiography, xii, 21, 36, 43, 67, 71, 93, 117
Hofstadter, Richard, 59
Holton, Woody, 112, 120–121, 125, 126–127, 128, 130
Horne, Gerald, 112
House of Burgesses, 127, 128
Hurston, Zora Neale, 113–114, 123
Hyman, Louis, 53

I

Île-à-Vache, 76, 77
illiberalism, 12, 54, 56, 57, 59, 60, 61. *See also* liberalism
import market, 15–16
individualism, 59
industrial revolution, 43, 45, 134–135
industrialization, 83, 135; American, 138–139; economic, 58; slave-based, 8
inequality, xiii, 2, 44, 59, 117, 121, 122
intermarriage, 14
Internal Revenue Service, 121, 139
internationalism, 55
interventionism, 58

J

Jamaica, 26, 27
James, C. L. R., 70 71
Jamestown, Virginia, xi, 97
Jim Crow, 61
Johnson, Walter, 54, 55, 67, 71

K

Kelley, Robin D. G., 131, 133, 136, 137, 138
Kendi, Ibram X., 112, 113
Keynes, John Maynard, 61
"King Cotton" thesis, 1–2, 5, 35, 49, 74, 117, 122, 131, 135, 139
Kock, Bernard, 76
Kruse, Kevin, 33
Kruse, Kevin M., 90

L

labor activism, 10, 60, 61, 137–138, 139
laissez-faire, 9, 14, 36, 57, 59, 60, 61, 122

164 | *Index*

Lee, Robert E., 130
Leggett, William, 14
Lewis, Cudjoe, 114
liberalism, classical, 45, 52, 53, 60–63. *See also*
    illiberalism
Liberator, The (abolitionist newspaper), 14
Liberty is Sweet (Holton), 129
Lincoln, Abraham, vii, xiii–xiv, 28–31, 66,
    73–80, 112–113, 120, 127, 130
List, Friedrich, 55
lullaby thesis, 29–30, 31

M
Magness, Phillip, 104
Mao Zedong, 138
market failures, 56, 60–61
Marler, Scott, 53
Marx, Karl, 122, 136, 139
Marxism, ix, 11, 70, 112, 131, 136, 138, 139
Mason, George, 129
McCloskey, Deirdre, 45
McPherson, James M., 23, 29, 65, 66, 70, 83,
    103, 119
Menard, John Willis, 77
mercantilism, 9, 10, 58, 60; imperial, 54–55;
    white supremacist, 55
Meyer, John R., 41, 136
Microsoft Excel, 37–38, 84, 116, 131, 132
Miles, Tiya, 33, 92
minimum wage laws, 61
Mitchell, James, 78, 79
Modern Monetary Theory, x, 143
Moreno, Paul, 137
Muhammad, Khalil Gibran, 33, 90

N
National Association for the Advancement of
    Colored People (NAACP), 138
National Socialism, 123, 139
nationalism, economic, 57
Neptune, H. Reuben, 71
New Deal, 51, 138
New History of Capitalism (NHC): and the
    1619 Project, 1, 36, 92, 111, 117–118; anti-
    capitalism and progressive history, 59–62;
    anti-capitalism as historical method,
    56–58; vs. classical liberalism, 45; critique
    of, xiii, 4–5, 71; divergent historical paths,
    46–52; faulty statistical claims, xii, 19, 21,
    22, 31–32, 50, 52; and the future of history

and capitalism, 62–63; historiographic dis-
    cussion, 43–46; and "King Cotton" thesis,
    131, 139; scholars associated with, 66–71;
    on slavery and capitalism, xii, 2–3, 9–10,
    12, 31–32, 33, 48, 53–55, 133, 136; support for
    teaching 1619 Project in K-12 classrooms,
    87; "whiteness" problem, 65–71
New York Draft Riots, 77
New York Mercantile Agency, 16–17
New York Times: and the 1619 Project, xi, 2,
    5, 9, 17, 23, 42, 65, 73, 82, 88, 90, 103, 105,
    106, 111, 113, 114, 123, 126, 132; avoiding
    debate over 1619 project, 87; claim of edi-
    torial rigor, 42; columnists, 106; dismissal
    of scholarly critics by, 81; edits to 1619
    essay, viii, 81–85, 89, 95, 96, 97, 99, 114,
    116, 126; selection of writers for 1619 proj-
    ect, 92. *See also* 1619 Project
NHC. *See* New History of Capitalism (NHC)
Nicolay, John, 76
Northwest Ordinance (1787), 27
Nunn, Nathan, 2

O
Oakes, James, 23, 29, 65, 66, 70, 103
Olmstead, Alan, 3–4, 20, 39–42, 50, 68, 117–118
Orwell, George, 99
Otis, James, 128

P
pacifism, 13
Panama, 78
Patten, Simon N., 61
Philipps, Wendell, 8
Phillips, Ulrich Bonnell, 135–136
political economy, 8, 49, 52, 60, 61
Pomeroy, Samuel, 78
population control, 61
Porto Bello plantation, 128
Potter, Claire, 106
presentism, 104, 105
private property, 46, 52, 133. *See also* property
    righrts
product safety regulations, 60
progressivism, 60–61
property rights, 54. *See also* private property
protectionism, 9; industrial, 55
Proud Family, The, 142
psychology, 61
Pulitzer Center, 87, 88
Pulitzer Prize, 65, 95, 114, 126

R

racial biology, 61
racial equality, 29
racism, 14, 69, 137, 138; historical, 59; institutional, 138; scientific, 61
Ransom, Roger, 69
redistribution, vii, 3, 10, 121, 123, 132, 142
redlining, 142
reparations, 19–22; and Coates, 3, 19; and Hannah-Jones, vii, x, xii, 89, 115, 138, 141–144
Republican Party, 31, 144
Rhode, Paul, 3–4, 20, 39–42, 50, 68, 117–118
Ricardo, David, 5, 8, 58
River of Dark Dreams (Johnson), 54
Rockman, Seth, 38, 53, 54, 66, 67, 131, 133–134
Roosevelt, Franklin Delano, 51
Rosenthal, Caitlin, 37–38, 116

S

Saez, Emmanuel, 117, 121
Say, Jean-Baptiste, 5, 8, 58
Schermerhorn, Calvin, 67
scientism, 60
segregation, xi, 56, 61
1776 Commission, 95
1776 Project, 84
Seward, William, 77, 79
Shapiro, Ben, 99
Silverstein, Jake, 23, 32, 33, 82, 84, 85, 89, 116, 118, 119
1619 Project: as activist/advocacy journalism, xii; and the American Revolution, 24–28, 81–85; anti-capitalism of, xiii, 9; articles and authors, 91; characterization of Lincoln, 28–31, critique of, 65–71, 69, 73, 89, 90, 92, 100, 103, 104–107, 113; debate over, 67–71; Desmond's problematic essay, 35–42; edits to 1619 vs. 1776 claim, viii, 95–101; expansion of, x; factual inconsistencies of, 23–34, 32–34, 88; inaccuracy of research, 17; inaccuracy of statistics, 3–4, 9, 20–21, 39–42; and "King Cotton" thesis, 135; lack of scholarly credibility, x, 87–90, 92–93, 96–97, 103, 113; and the NHC, 2; as opinion/advocacy journalism, 88–89; rebuttals of, vii; on slavery and capitalism, 31–32, 139; suitability for K-12 classrooms, xii, 87–93; "whiteness" problem, 84
1619 Project Hulu docuseries, viii, ix–x; "Capitalism" episode, 131–140; final episode

(reparations), 141–144; first episode (Williamsburg), x, 125–130
1619 Project, The: A New Origin Story, viii, ix, 112, 113, 114–123
slave narratives, 4, 41
slavery: abolition of, 27; and the American Revolution, ix, xiii, 24–28, 73, 74, 81–85, 89, 92, 97, 111, 112, 118–121, 125–130; Ancient Roman, 133; anti-capitalist ideology of, 7–12; atonement for, 10; in the Bahamas, 26; in Britain, 129–130; and capitalism, vii, xiii, 5, 17–18, 21–22, 24, 31–32, 38–39, 42, 47, 50, 53–58, 60, 62, 65, 68, 70, 71, 99, 115, 117, 122, 133–134; economic importance of, 21–22; defense of, 8, 10, 12, 22, 120; economics of, ix, 5, 32, 33, 47–48, 50, 67, 69, 83, 89, 90, 111, 119, 131; efficiency of, 50; in England, 24–25, 27–28, 82, 119; history of, xi, xiii, 22, 33, 47–48, 68, 69, 70, 87, 90, 92, 100–101, 106, 114; in Jamaica, 26; legacy of, x, 2–3, 5, 10, 22, 113–114, 117, 122, 131, 139; Marx's rejection of, 11; and modern management, 3, 4, 31, 36–37, 116; plantation, 1, 2, 5, 9, 11, 37, 48, 50, 65; in public school curricula, 87–93; as socialism, 11; socio-economic dimensions of, 44; supposed necessity of, 2, 19; unprofitability thesis, 135–136; and US economics, 3; and the use of torture, 3, 40, 41, 117–118; in the West Indies, 25, 26, 27, 57
Slavery Abolition Act (1833), 26
slaves: colonization of, vii, xiii–xiv, 28–31, 66, 72–80, 112–113; fugitive, 17; liberation of, 25, 27, 28, 82, 120–121, 126–127, 129, 130
Smith, Adam, 5, 8, 52, 55–56, 58, 62
Soave, Robby, 96
social Darwinism, 59, 61
social history, 46–47
social justice, 10, 106
socialism, 11, 12, 37, 136; democratic, 122; in the United States, 122–123
Sociology for the South (Fitzhugh), 8
Sombart, Werner, 123, 139
Somerset v. Stewart, 24, 25, 27, 120, 130
Soviet Union, 37
Spencer, Herbert, 59
Spooner, Lysander, 17
Stalin, Joseph, 138
Stamped from the Beginning (Kendi), 113
Stampp, Kenneth, 68
Stephens, Bret, 96

166 | *Index*

Stevens, Thaddeus, 78–79
Sullivan, Andrew, 114
Sumner, Charles, 8
surplus value, 11
Sutch, Richard, 69
Sweet, James H., 104–109

T

Tappan, Arthur, 13–14
Tappan, Lewis, 13–14, 15–16, 18
Tappan Riots, 13–14
tariff targeting, 60
Tarleton, Banastre, 26
taxation, xi, 31, 60, 121–122, 123, 126, 139, 142, 143
Taylor, Alan, 120
Time on the Cross, The (Fogel & Engerman), 47, 69
Treasury Department, 121
Trump, Donald, viii, 88, 93, 95, 115
trust-busting, 60

U

Unconstitutionality of Slavery, The (Spooner), 17
Underground Railroad, 17
unemployment, 59
United States: economic growth of, 31–32, 39–40; gross domestic product (GDP), 4, 9, 19, 20, 21, 22, 50, 134, 142; slave states vs. free states, 27
US Constitution: 13th Amendment, 79; 16th Amendment, 122; and slavery, xi
Usher, John Palmer, 78

V

von Mises, Ludwig, 61

W

Wagner Act, 138
Waldstreicher, David, 112
Walker, Quock, 27
Walsh, David Austin, 106
Washington, George, 121, 129
Wealth of Nations (Smith), 52, 55
Welles, Gideon, 80
Wells, Ida Bae, 98, 106
West Indies, 25, 26, 27, 30, 57, 71, 76, 119
White Rage (Anderson), 21
white supremacy, 55, 77, 80
Wigfall, Louis T., 1, 2
Wilberforce, William, 26
Wilentz, Sean, 23, 29, 74, 76, 78, 80, 103
William, HMS, 127
Williams, Eric, 70, 71
Williamsburg, Virginia, 125, 126, 127, 129, 130
Wilson, Woodrow, 61
Wood, Gordon, 23, 65, 66, 70, 83, 119
work hour regulations, 60, 61
World Socialist Web Site (WSWS), 103, 104
Wright, Gavin, 69, 134

Y

Young, Cathy, 83

Z

Zucman, Gabriel, 117, 121

About the Author

PHILLIP W. MAGNESS is a research fellow and the David J. Theroux Chair in Political Economy at Independent Institute. His work includes the economic dimensions of slavery in the United States and Caribbean world, as well as other aspects of economic history. He holds a PhD and MPP from George Mason University's School of Public Policy.